PREDESTINATION CALM]

BY

John Wesley

PREDESTINATION CALMLY CONSIDERED

Published by Scriptura Press

New York City, NY

First published circa 1791

ABOUT SCRIPTURA PRESS

Scriptura Press is a Christian company that makes Christian works available and affordable to all. We are a non-denominational publishing group that shares the teachings of the Scripture, whether in the form of sermons or histories of the Church.

Predestination Calmly Considered

1. I AM inclined to believe, that many of those who enjoy the "faith which worketh by love," may remember some time when the power of the Highest wrought upon them in an eminent manner; when the voice of the Lord laid the mountains low, brake all the rocks in pieces, and mightily shed abroad his love in their hearts, by the Holy Ghost given unto them. And at that time it is certain they had no power to resist the grace of God. They were then no more able to stop the course of that torrent which carried all before it, than to stem the waves of the sea with their hand, or to stay the sun in the midst of heaven.

2. And the children of God may continually observe how his love leads them on from faith to faith; with what tenderness He watches over their souls; with what care He brings them back if they go astray, and then upholds their going in his path, that their footsteps may not slide. They cannot but observe how unwilling He is to let them go from serving him; and how, notwithstanding the stubbornness of their wills, and the wildness of their passions, he goes on in his work, conquering and to conquer, till he hath put all his enemies under his feet.

3. The farther this work is carried on in their hearts, the more earnestly do they cry out, "Not unto us, O Lord, but unto thy name give the praise, for thy mercy and for thy truth's sake!" the more deeply are they convinced that "by grace we are saved, not of works, lest any man should boast;" that we are not pardoned and accepted with God for the sake of anything we have done, but wholly and solely for the sake of Christ, of what he hath done and suffered for us; the more assuredly likewise do they know, that the condition of this acceptance is faith alone; before which gift of God no good work can be done, none which hath not in it the nature of sin.

4. How easily then may a believer infer, from what he hath experienced in his own soul, that the true grace of God always works irresistibly in every believer! that God will finish wherever he has begun this work, so that it is impossible for any believer to fall from grace! and, lastly, that the reason why God gives this to some only and not to others, is, because, of his own will, without any previous regard either to their faith or works, he hath absolutely, unconditionally, predestined them to life, before the foundation of the world!

5. Agreeable hereto, in "The Protestant Confession of faith," drawn up at Paris, in the year 1559, we have these words: —

"We believe, that out of the general corruption and condemnation in which all men are plunged, God draws those whom, in his eternal and unalterable counsel, he has elected by his own goodness and mercy, through our Lord Jesus Christ, without considering their works, leaving the others in the same corruption and condemnation." (Article 12.)

6. To the same effect speak the Dutch Divines, assembled at Dort in the year 1618. Their words are: —

"Whereas, in process of time, God bestowed faith on some, and not on others, — this proceeds from his eternal decree; according to which, he softens the hearts of the elect, and leaveth them that are not elect in their wickedness and hardness.

"And herein is discovered the difference put between men equally lost; that is to say, the decree of election and reprobation.

"Election is the unchangeable decree of God, by which, before the foundation of the world, he hath chosen in Christ unto salvation a set number of men. This election is one and the same of all wish are to be saved.

"Not all men are elected, but some not elected; whom God, in his unchangeable good pleasure, hath decreed to leave in the common misery, and not to bestow saving faith upon them; but leaving them in their own ways, at last to condemn and punish them everlastingly, for their unbelief, and also for their other sins. And this is the decree of reprobation." (Article 6, et seq.)

7. Likewise in "The Confession of Faith" set forth by the Assembly of English and Scotch Divines, in the year 1646, are these words: —

"God from all eternity did unchangeably ordain whatsoever comes to pass.

"By the decree of God, for the manifestation of his glory, some men and angels are predestined unto everlasting life, and others fore-ordained to everlasting death.

"These angels and men thus predestined and fore-ordained are particularly and unchangeably designed, and their number so certain and definite that it cannot be either increased or diminished.

"Those of mankind that are predestined unto life, God, before the foundation of the world, hath chosen in Christ unto everlasting glory, without any foresight of faith or good works.

"The rest of mankind God was pleased, for the glory of his sovereign power over his creatures, to pass by, and to ordain them to dishonor and wrath." (Chapter 3.)

No less express are Mr. Calvin's words, in his "Christian Institutions:"—

"All men are not created for the same end; but some are fore-ordained to eternal life, others to eternal damnation. So according as every man was created for the one end or the other, we say, he was elected, that is, predestined to life, or reprobated, that is, predestined to damnation." (Cap. 21, sec. 1.)

8. Indeed there are some who assert the decree of election, and not the decree of reprobation. They assert that God hath, by a positive, unconditional decree, chosen some to life and salvation; but not that he hath by any such decree devoted the rest of mankind to destruction. These are they to whom I would address myself first. And let me beseech you, brethren, by the mercies of God, to lift up your hearts to him, and to beg of him to free you from all prepossession, from the prejudices even of your tender years, and from whatsoever might hinder the light of God from shining in upon your souls. Let us calmly and fairly weigh these things in the balance of the sanctuary. And let all be done in love and meekness of Wisdom, as becomes those who are fighting under one Captain, and who humbly hope they are joint-heirs through him of the glory which shall be revealed.

I am verily persuaded, that, in the uprightness of your hearts, you defend the decree of unconditional election; even in the same uprightness wherein you reject and abhor that of unconditional reprobation. But consider, I intreat you, whether you are consistent with yourselves; consider, whether this election can be separate from reprobation; whether one of them does not imply the other, so that, in holding one, you must hold both.

9. That this was the judgment of those who had the most deeply considered the nature of these decrees, of the Assembly of English and Scotch Divines, of the Reformed Churches both in France and the Low Countries, and of Mr. Calvin himself, appears from their own words, beyond all possibility of contradiction. "Out of the general corruption," saith the French Church, "he draws those whom he hath elected; leaving the others in the same corruption, according to his immovable decree." "By the decree of God," says the Assembly of English and Scotch Divines, "some are predestinated unto everlasting life, others fore-ordained to everlasting death." "God hath once for all," saith Mr. Calvin, "appointed, by an eternal and unchangeable decree, to whom he would give salvation and whom he would devote to destruction." (Inst., cap. 3, sec. 7.) Nay, it is observable, Mr. Calvin speaks with utter contempt and disdain of all who endeavor to separate one from the other, who assert election without reprobation. "Many," says he, "as it were to excuse God, own election, and deny reprobation. But this is quite silly and childish. For election cannot stand without reprobation. Whom God passes by,

those he reprobates. It is one and the same thing." (Inst., 1. 3, c. 23, sec. 1.)

10. Perhaps upon deeper consideration, you will find yourself of the same judgment. It may be, you also hold reprobation, though you know it not;. Do not you believe, that God who made "one vessel unto honor," hath made "another unto" eternal "dishonor?" Do not you believe, that the men who "turn the grace of our God into lasciviousness, were before ordained of God unto this condemnation?" Do not you think, that for "this same purpose God raised Pharaoh up, that he might show his sovereign power in his destruction?" and that "Jacob have I loved, but Esau have I hated," refers to their eternal state? Why, then, you hold absolute reprobation, and you think Esau and Pharaoh were instances of it, as well as all those "vessels made unto dishonor," those men "before ordained into condemnation."

11. To set this matter in a still clearer light, you need only answer one question: Is any man saved who is not elected? Is it possible, that any not elected should be saved? If you say, "No," you put an end to the doubt. You espouse election and reprobation together. You confirm Mr. Calvin's words, that "without reprobation, election itself cannot stand." You allow, (though you was not sensible of it before,) that "whom God elects not, them he reprobates."

Try whether it be possible, in any particular case, to separate election from reprobation. Take one of those who are supposed not to be elected; one whom God hath not chosen unto life and salvation. Can this man be saved from sin and hell? You answer, "No." Why not? "Because he is not elected. Because God hath unchangeably decreed to save so many souls, and no more; and he is not of that number. Him God hath decreed to pass by; to leave him to everlasting destruction; in consequence of which irresistible decree, the man perishes everlastingly." O, my brethren, how small is the difference between this, and a broad, barefaced reprobation!

12. Let me intreat you to make this case your own. In the midst of life, you are in death; your soul is dead while you live, if you live in sin, if you do not live to God. And who can deliver you from the body of this death? Only the grace of God in Jesus Christ our Lord. But God hath decreed to give this grace to others only, and not to you; to leave you in unbelief and spiritual death, and for that unbelief to punish you with death everlasting. Well then mayest thou cry, even till thy throat is dry, "O wretched man that I am!" For an unchangeable, irresistible decree standeth between thee and the very possibility of salvation. Go now and find out how to split the hair between thy being reprobated and not elected; how to separate

reprobation, in its most effectual sense, from unconditional election!

13. Acknowledge then that you hold reprobation. Avow it in the face of the sun. To be consistent with yourself, you must openly assert, that "without reprobation this election cannot stand." You know it cannot. You know, if God hath fixed a decree that these men only shall be saved, in such a decree it is manifestly implied, that all other men shall be damned. If God hath decreed that this part of mankind, and no more, shall live eternally, you cannot but see it is therein decreed, that the other part shall never see life. O let us deal ingenuously with each other! What we really hold, let us openly profess. And if reprobation be the truth, it will bear the light; for "the word of our God shall stand forever."

14. Now then, without any extenuation on the one hand, or exaggeration on the other, let us look upon this doctrine, call it what you please, naked and in its native color. Before the foundations of the world were laid, God of his own mere will and pleasure fixed a decree concerning all the children of men why should be born unto the end of the world. This decree was unchangeable with regard to God, and irresistible with regard to man. And herein it was ordained, that one part of mankind should be saved from sin and hell, and all the rest left to perish forever and ever, without help, without hope. That none of these should have that grace which alone could prevent their dwelling with everlasting burnings, God decreed, for this cause alone, "because it was his good pleasure;" and for this end, "to show forth his glorious power, and his sovereignty over all the earth."

15. Now, can you, upon reflection, believe this? Perhaps you will say, "I do not think about it." That will never do. You not only think about it, (though it may be confusedly,) but speak about it too, whenever you speak of unconditional election. You do not think about it! What do you mean? Do you never think about Esau or Pharaoh? or, in general, about a certain number of souls whom alone God hath decreed to save? Why, in that; very thought reprobation lurks; it entered your heart the moment that entered: It stays as long as that stays; and you cannot speak that thought, without speaking of reprobation. True, it is covered with fig-leaves, so that a heedless eye may not observe it to be there. But, if you narrowly observe, unconditional election cannot appear without the cloven foot of reprobation.

16. "But do not the Scriptures speak of election? They say, St. Paul was 'an elected or chosen vessel;' nay, and speak of great numbers of men as 'elect according to the foreknowledge of God.' You cannot, therefore, deny there is such a thing as election. And, if there is, what do you mean by it?" I will tell you, in all plainness and simplicity. I believe it commonly means

one of these two things: First, a divine appointment of some particular men, to do some particular work in the world. And this election I believe to be not only personal, but absolute and unconditional. Thus Cyrus was elected to rebuild the temple, and St. Paul, with the twelve, to preach the gospel. But I do not find this to have any necessary connection with eternal happiness. Nay, it is plain it has not; for one who is elected in this sense lay yet be lost eternally. "Have I not chosen" (elected) "you twelve?" saith our Lord; "yet one of you hath a devil." Judas, you see, was elected as well as the rest; yet is his lot with the devil and his angels.

17. I believe election means, Secondly, a divine appointment of some men to eternal happiness. But I believe this election to be conditional, as well as the reprobation opposite thereto. I believe the eternal decree concerning both is expressed in those words: "He that believeth shall be saved; he that believeth not shall be damned." And this decree, without doubt, God will not change, and man cannot resist. According to this, all true believers are in Scripture termed elect, as all who continue in unbelief are so long properly reprobates, that is, unapproved of God, and without discernment touching the things of the Spirit.

18. Now, God, to whom all things are present at once, who sees all eternity at one view, "calleth the things that are not as though they were;" the things that are not yet as though they were now subsisting. Thus he calls Abraham the "father of many nations," before even Isaac was born. And thus Christ is called "the Lamb slain from the foundation of the world;" though he was not slain, in fact, till some thousand years after. In like manner, God calleth true believers, "elect from the foundation of the world;" although they were not actually elect, or believers, till many ages after, in their several generations. Then only it was that they were actually elected, when they were made the "sons of God by faith." Then were they, in fact, "chosen and taken out of the world; elect," saith St. Paul, "through belief of the truth;" or, as St. Peter expresses it, "elect according to the foreknowledge of God, through sanctification of the Spirit."

19. This election I as firmly believe, as I believe the Scripture to be of God. But unconditional election I cannot believe; not only because I cannot find it in Scripture, but also (to wave all other considerations) because it necessarily implies unconditional reprobation. Find out any election which does not imply reprobation, and I will gladly agree to it. But reprobation I can never agree to while I believe the Scripture to be of God; as being utterly irreconcilable to the whole scope and tenor both of the Old and New Testament.

O that God would give me the desire of my heart! that he would grant the thing which I long for I even that your mind might now be free and calm, and open to the light of his Spirit! that you would impartially consider how it is possible to reconcile reprobation with the following Scriptures:

—

"Because thou hast eaten of the tree of which I commanded thee, saying, Thou shalt; not eat of it; in the sweat of thy face shalt thou eat bread." (Genesis 3:17.) The curse shall come on thee and thine offspring, not because of any absolute decree of mine, but because of thy sin.

"If thou doest well, shalt thou not be accepted? And if thou doest not well, sin lieth at the door." (Genesis 4:7.) Sin only, not the decree of reprobation, hinders thy being accepted.

"Know that the Lord thy God, he is the faithful God, which keepeth covenant and mercy with them that love him and keep his commandments to a thousand generations; and repayeth them that hate him to their face, to destroy them. Wherefore, if ye hearken to these judgments, and keep, and do them, the Lord thy God shall keep unto thee the covenant which he sware unto thy fathers." (Deuteronomy 7:9, 12.) "Behold, I set before you this day a blessing and a curse; a blessing, if you obey the commandments of the Lord your God; and a curse, if you will not obey." (11:26, 27, 28.)

"See, I have set before thee this day life and good, and death and evil; in that I command thee this day to love the Lord thy God to walk in his ways, and to keep his commandments, and the Lord thy God shall bless thee. But if thou wilt not hear, I denounce unto you this day, that ye shall surely perish. I call heaven and earth to record this day, that I have set before you life and death, blessing and cursing. Therefore, choose life, that both thou and thy seed may live." (30:15, etc.)

"And the Spirit of God came upon Azariah, and he said, The Lord is with you while ye be with him; and if ye seek him, he will be found of you; but if ye forsake him he will forsake you." (2 Chronicles 15:1, 2.)

"After all that is come upon us, for our evil deeds, and for our great trespass; should we again break thy commandments, wouldest thou not be angry with us, till thou hadst consumed us? "(Ezra 9:13, 14.)

"Behold, God is mighty, and despiseth not any." (Job 36:5.) Could he then reprobate any?

"The Lord is good to all: And his tender mercies are over all his works." (Psalm 145:9.)

"Turn you at my reproof: Behold, I will pour out my Spirit unto you. Because I have called, and ye refused; I have stretched out my hand, and no man regarded: I also will laugh at your calamity, I will mock when your fear cometh. Then shall they call upon me, but I will not answer; they shall seek me early, but they shall not find me." (Proverbs 1:23, etc.) Why? because of my decree? No; but "because they hated knowledge, and did not choose the fear of the Lord."

"I have spread out my hands all the day unto a rebellious people; a people that provoked me to anger continually to my face. Therefore will I measure their former work into their bosom. Ye shall all bow down to the slaughter; because when I called, ye did not answer. Therefore, ye shall leave your name for a curse unto my chosen; for the Lord God shall slay thee, and call his servants by another name." (Isaiah 65:2, etc.)

"The soul that sinneth, it shall die. The son shall not bear" (eternally) "the iniquity of the father, neither shall the father bear the iniquity of the son. Have I any pleasure at all that the wicked should die? saith the Lord; and not that he should return from his ways, and live?" (Ezekial 18:20, 23.)

"Every one that heareth these sayings of mine, and doeth them not, shall be likened unto a foolish man, which built his house upon the sand." (Matthew 7:26.) Nay, he could not help it, if he was ordained thereto.

"Then began he to upbraid the cities wherein most of his mighty works were done, because they repented not. Who unto thee, Chorazin! Wo unto thee, Bethsaida! For if the mighty works which were done in you, had been done in Tyre and Sidon, they would have repented long ago in sackcloth and ashes." (What, if they were not elected? And if they of Bethsaida had been elected, would they not have repented too?)

"Therefore I say unto you, It shall be more tolerable for Tyre and Sidon in the day of judgment than for you. And thou, Capernaum, which art exalted unto heaven, shalt be brought down to hell. For if the mighty works which have been done in thee, had been done in Sodom, it would have remained until this day. But I say unto you, It shall be more tolerable for the land of Sodom in the day of judgment than for thee." (Matthew 11:20, etc.)

"The men of Nineveh shall rise in judgment with this generation, and shall condemn it: Because they repented at the preaching of Jonas; and, behold, a greater than Jonas is here." (12:41.) But what was this to the purpose, if the men of Nineveh were elected, and this generation of men were not?

"It is given unto you to know the mysteries of the kingdom of heaven, but unto them it is not given. For whosoever hath," (that is, uses what he hath,) "to him shall be given, and he shall have more abundance: But whosoever hath not, from him shall be taken away even that he hath." (13:11, 12.)

"They which were called were not worthy," (22:8,) were shut out from the marriage of the Lamb: — Why so? Because "they would not come." (Verse 3.)

The whole twenty-fifth chapter requires, and will reward, your most serious consideration. If you can reconcile unconditional reprobation with this, you may reconcile it with the eighteenth of Ezekiel.

"This is the condemnation, that light is come into the world, and men love" (or choose) "darkness rather than light." (John 3:19.)

"How can ye believe, who receive honor one of another, and seek not the honor that cometh of God?" (5:44.) Observe the reason why they could not believe: It is not in God, but in themselves.

"Thy money perish with thee!" (And so doubtless it did.) "Thou hast neither part nor lot in this matter; for thy heart is not right in the sight of God. Repent therefore of this thy wickedness, and pray God, if perhaps the thought of thine heart may be forgiven thee." (Acts 8:20, etc.) So that St. Peter had no thought of any absolute reprobation even in the case of Simon Magus.

"They are without excuse; because when they knew God, they glorified him not as God — wherefore God also gave them up to uncleanness — who changed the truth of God into a lie. — For this cause God gave them up to vile affections. — As they did not like to retain God in their knowledge, God gave them over to a reprobate mind, to do those things which are not convenient." (Romans 1:20, etc.)

"Them that perish, because they received not the love of the truth, that they might be saved. And for this cause God shall send them strong delusion, to believe a lie; that they all might be damned who believed not the truth, but had pleasure in unrighteousness." (2 Thessolonians 2:10, etc.)

20. How will you reconcile reprobation with the following scriptures, which declare God's willingness that all should be saved?

"As many as ye shall find, bid" (invite) "to the marriage." (Matthew 22:9.)

"Go ye into all the world, and preach the gospel to every creature." (Mark 16:15.)

"And when he came near, he beheld the city, and wept over it, saying, If" (rather, O that) "thou hadst known, at least in this thy day, the things which belong unto thy peace!" (Luke 19:41, etc.)

"These things I say, that ye may be saved," (John 5:34,) viz., those who persecuted him, and "sought to slay him," (verse 16,) and of whom he complains, "Ye will not come unto me, that ye may have life." (Verse 40.)

"God that made the world and all things therein — giveth to all life, and breath, and all things, and hath made of one blood all nations of men, for to dwell on all the face of the earth — That they should seek the Lord."

(Acts 17:24.) Observe, this was God's end in creating all nations on all the earth.

"As by the offense of one, judgment came upon all men to condemnation; so by the righteousness of one the free gift came upon all men unto justification of life." (Romans 5:18.) "The same Lord over all is rich" (in mercy) "unto all that call upon him." (10:12.)

"This is good and acceptable in the sight of God our Savior; who willeth all men to be saved." (1 Timothy 2:3, 4.) "Who is the Savior of all men, especially of those that believe;" (6:10;) that is, intentionally of all, and actually of believers.

"If any man lack wisdom, let him ask of God, who giveth to all men liberally, and upbraideth not." (James 1:5.)

"The Lord is longsuffering toward us, not willing that any should perish, but that all should come to repentance." (2 Peter 3:9.)

"We have seen and do testify that the Father sent the Son to be the Savior of the world." (1 John 4:14)

21. How will you reconcile reprobation with the following scriptures, which declare that Christ came to save all men; that he died for all; that he atoned for all, even for those that finally perish?

"The Son of man is come to save that which is lost," (Matthew 18:11,) without any restriction.

"Behold the Lamb of God, which taketh away the sin of the world." (John 1:29) "God sent his Son into the world, that the world through him might be saved." (3:17.) "I came not" (now) "to judge the world, but to save the world." (12:47.)

"Destroy not him with thy meat, for whom Christ died." (Romans 14:15.) "Through thy knowledge shall thy weak brother perish, for whom, Christ died." (1 Corinthians 8:11.)

"We thus judge, that if one died for all, then were all dead; and that he died for all, that those" (or all) "who live should live unto Him which died for them." (2 Corinthians 5:14, etc.) Here you see, not only that Christ died for all men, but likewise the end of his dying for them.

"Christ Jesus, who gave himself a ransom for all." (1 Timothy 2:6.)

"We see Jesus made lower than the angels, that he might taste death for every man." (Hebrews 2:9.)

"There shall be false teachers among you, who shall privately bring in damnable heresies, even denying the Lord that bought them, and bring upon themselves swift destruction." (2 Peter 2:1.) You see he bought or redeemed even those that perish, that bring upon themselves swift destruction.

"If any man sin, we have an Advocate with the Father, Jesus Christ the righteous; and he is the propitiation for our sins" (who are elect, according to the knowledge of God) "and not for ours only, but also for the sins of the whole world." (1 John 2:1, 2.)

You are sensible, these are but a very small part of the scriptures which might be brought on each of these heads. But they are enough; and they require no comment: Taken in their plain, easy, and obvious sense, they abundantly prove, that there is not, cannot be, any such thing as unconditional reprobation.

22. But to be a little more particular: How can you possibly reconcile reprobation with those scriptures that declare the justice of God? To cite one for all:

"What mean ye that ye use this proverb, The fathers have eaten sour grapes, and the children's teeth are set on edge? As I live, saith the Lord, ye shall not have occasion any more to use this proverb in Israel. Behold, all souls are mine; as the soul of the father, so the soul of the son is mine;" (and however I may temporally visit the sins of the fathers upon the children, yet this visitation extends no farther; but) "the soul that sinneth, it shall die," for its own sin, and not another's. "But if a man be just, and do that which is lawful and right, he shall surely live, saith the Lord God. If he beget a son which is a robber, shall he then live? He shall not live, — he shall surely die. Yet say ye, Why? doth not the son bear the iniquity of the father?" (Temporally he doth, as in the case of Achan, Korah, and a thousand others; but not eternally.) When the son hath done that which is lawful and right, he shall surely live. The soul that sinneth, it shall die; "shall die the second death." The son shall not bear the iniquity of the father, neither shall the father bear the iniquity of the son. The righteousness of the righteous shall be upon him, and the wickedness of the wicked shall be upon him. Yet ye say, The way of the Lord is not equal. Hear now, O Israel. Is not my way equal?" (equitable, just?) "Are not your ways unequal? When a righteous man turneth away from his righteousness, and committeth iniquity, and dieth in them, for his iniquity that he hath done shall he die. Again, when the wicked man turneth away from his wickedness that he hath committed, and doeth that which is lawful and right, he shall save his soul alive. Therefore I will judge you, O house of Israel, every one according to his ways, saith the Lord God. Repent, and turn yourselves from all your transgressions. So iniquity shall not be your ruin." (Ezekiel 18:2, etc.)

Through this whole passage God is pleased to appeal to man himself touching the justice of His proceedings. And well might he appeal to our own conscience, according to the account of them which is here given. But it is an account which all the art of man will never reconcile with unconditional reprobation.

23. Do you think it will cut the knot to say, "Why, if God might justly have passed by all men," (speak out, "If God might justly have reprobated all men,"— for it comes to the same point,) "then he may justly pass by some: But God might justly have passed by all men?" Are you sure he might? Where is it written? I cannot find it in the word of God. Therefore I reject it as a bold, precarious assertion, utterly unsupported by Holy Scripture.

If you say, "But you know in your own conscience, God might justly have passed by you:" I deny it. That God might justly, for my unfaithfulness to his grace, have given me up long ago, I grant: But this concession supposes me to have had that grace which you say a reprobate never had.

But besides, in making this supposition, of what God might have justly done, you suppose his justice might have been separate from his other attributes, from his mercy in particular. But this never was, nor ever will be; nor indeed is it possible it should. All his attributes are inseparably joined: They cannot be divided, no, not for a moment. Therefore this whole argument stands, not only on an unscriptural, but on an absurd, impossible supposition.

24. Do you say, "Nay, but it is just for God to pass by whom he will, because of his sovereignty; for he saith himself, 'May not I do what I will with my own?' and, 'Hath not the potter power over his own clay?'" I answer, The former of these sentences stands in the conclusion of that parable, (Matthew 20) wherein our Lord reproves the Jews for murmuring at God's giving the same reward to the Gentiles as to them. To one of these murmurers it is that God says, "Friend, I do thee no wrong. Take that thine is, and go thy way. I will give unto this last even as unto thee." Then follows: "Is it not lawful for me to do what I will with mine own? Is thine eye evil, because I am good?" As if he had said, "May I not give my own kingdom to whom I please? Art thou angry because I am merciful?" It is then undeniably clear, that God does not here assert a right of reprobating any man. Here is nothing spoken of reprobation, bad or good. Here is no kind of reference thereto. This text therefore has nothing to do with the conclusion it was brought to prove.

25. But you add: "Hath not the potter power over his own clay?" Let us consider the context of these words also. They are found in the ninth chapter of the Epistle to the Romans; an Epistle, the general scope and

intent of which is, to publish the eternal, unchangeable proqesiv, purpose or decree of God, "He that believeth, shall be saved: He that believeth not shall be damned." The justice of God in condemning those that believed not, and the necessity of believing in order to salvation, the Apostle proves at large in the three first chapters, which he confirms in the fourth by the example of Abraham. In the former part of the fifth and in the sixth chapter, he describes the happiness and holiness of true believers. (The latter part of the fifth is a digression, concerning the extent of the benefits flowing from the death of Christ.) In the seventh he shows in what sense believers in Christ are delivered from the law; and describes the miserable bondage of those who are still under the law; that is, who are truly convinced of sin, but not able to conquer it. In the eighth he again describes the happy liberty of those who truly believe in Christ; and encourages them to suffer for the faith, as by other considerations, so by this in particular, "We know that all things work together for good to them that love God, to them that are called" (by the preaching of his word) "according to his purpose," (verse 28,) or decree, unalterably fixed from eternity, "He that believeth shall be saved." "For whom he did fore know" as believing, "he also did predestinate to be conformed to the image of his Son. Moreover, whom he did predestinate, them he also called," by his word; (so that term is usually taken in St. Paul's Epistles;) "and whom he called, them he also justified;" (the word is here taken in its wildest sense, as including sanctification also;) "and whom he justified, them he glorified." Thence to the end of the chapter, he strongly encourages all those who had the love of God shed abroad in their hearts, to have a good hope, that no sufferings should ever "be able to separate them from the loves of God which is in Christ Jesus."

26. But as the Apostle was aware how deeply the Jews were offended at the whole tenor of his doctrine, and more especially at his asserting,

(1.)That the Jews themselves could not; be saved without believing in Jesus; and,

(2.)That the Heathens by believing in him might partake of the same salvation; he spends the whole ninth chapter upon them;

Wherein,

(1.)He declares the tender love he had for them. (Verses 1-3.)

(2) Allows the great national privileges they enjoyed above any people under heaven. (Verses 4, 5.)

(3.)Answers their grand objection to his doctrine, taken from the justice of God to their fathers. (Verses 6-13.)

(4.)Removes another objection, taken from the justice of God;

interweaving all along strong reproofs to the Jews, for priding
themselves on those privileges which were owing merely to the
good pleasure of God, not to their fathers' goodness, any more
than their own. (Verses 14-23.)

(5.)Resumes and proves by Scripture his former assertion, that many
Jews would be lost, and many Heathens saved. (Verses 24-29.)
And, lastly, sums up the general drift of this chapter, and indeed of
the whole Epistle. "What shall we say then?" What is the
conclusion from the whole? the sum of all which has been spoken?
Why, that many Gentiles already partake of the great salvation,
and many Jews fall short of it. Wherefore? Because they would not
receive it by faith. And whosoever believeth not, cannot be saved;
whereas, "whosoever believeth in Christ," whether Jew or Gentile,
"shall not be ashamed." (Verses 30-33.)

27. Those words, "Hath not the potter power over his own clay?" are part
of St. Paul's answer to that objection, That it was unjust for God to show
that mercy to the Gentiles which he withheld from his own people. This
he first simply denies, saying, "God forbid!" And then observes, that,
according to his own words to Moses, God has a right to fix the terms on
which he will show mercy, which neither the will nor the power of man
can alter; (verses 15, 16;) and to withdraw his mercy from them who, like
Pharaoh, will not comply with those terms. (Verse 17.) And that
accordingly "he hath mercy on whom he will have mercy," namely, those
that truly believe; "and whom he will," namely, obstinate unbelievers, he
suffers to be "hardened."

28. But "why then," say the objectors, "doth he find fault" with those
that are hardened? "for who hath resisted his will?" (Verse 19.) To this
insolent misconstruction of what he had said, the Apostle first gives a
severe rebuke; and then adds, "Shall the thing formed say unto him that
formed it, Why hast thou made me thus?" Why hast thou made me
capable of salvation only on those terms? None indeed hath resisted this
will of God. "He that believeth not, shall be damned." But is this any
ground for arraigning his justice? "Hath not" the great "Potter power over
his own clay to make," or appoint, one sort of "vessels," namely,
believers, "to honor, and" the others "to dishonor?" Hath he not a right to
distribute eternal honor and dishonor, on whatever terms he pleases?
especially, considering the goodness and patience he shows, even towards
them that believe not; considering that when they have provoked him "to
show his wrath, and to make the power" of his vengeance "known, yet" he
"endures, with much longsuffering," even those "vessels of wrath," who

had before "fitted" themselves "to destruction." There is then no more room to reply against God, for making his vengeance known on those vessels of wrath, than for "making known" his glorious love "on the vessels of mercy whom he had before" by faith "prepared for glory; even us, whom he hath called, not of the Jews only, but also of the Gentiles."

29. I have spoken more largely than I designed, in order to show, that neither our Lord, in the above-mentioned parable, nor St. Paul, in these words, had any view to God's sovereign power, as the ground of unconditional reprobation. And beware you go no further therein, than you are authorized by them. Take care, whenever you speak of these high things, to "speak as the oracles of God." And if so, you will never speak of the sovereignty of God, but in conjunction with his other attributes. For the Scripture nowhere speaks of this single attribute, as separate from the rest. Much less does it anywhere speak of the sovereignty of God as singly disposing the eternal states of men. No, no; in this awful work, God proceeds according to the known rules of his justice and mercy; but never assigns his sovereignty as the cause why any man is punished with everlasting destruction.

30. Now then, are you not quite out of your way? You are not in the way which God hath revealed. You are putting eternal happiness and misery on an unscriptural and a very dreadful footing. Make the case your own: Here are you, a sinner, convinced that you deserve the damnation of hell. Sorrow, therefore, and fear have filled your heart. And how shall you be comforted? By the promises of God? But perhaps you have no part therein; for they belong only to the elect. By the consideration of his love and tender mercy? But what are these to you, if you are a reprobate? God does not love you at all; you, like Esau, he hath hated even from eternity. What ground then can you have for the least shadow of hope? Why, it is possible, (that is all,) that God's sovereign will may be on your side. Possibly God may save you, because he will! O poor encouragement to despairing sinners! I fear "faith" rarely "cometh by hearing" this!

31. The sovereignty of God is then never to be brought to supersede his justice. And this is the present objection against unconditional reprobation; (the plain consequence of unconditional election;) it flatly contradicts, indeed utterly overthrows, the Scripture account of the justice of God. This has been proved in general already; let us now weigh a few particulars. And, (1.) The Scripture describes God as the Judge of the earth. But how shall God in justice judge the world? (O consider this, as in the presence of God, with reverence and godly fear!) How shall God in justice judge the world, if there be any decree of reprobation? On this

supposition, what should those on the left hand be condemned for? For their having done evil? They could not help it. There never was a time when they could have helped it. God, you say, "of old ordained them to this condemnation." And "who hath resisted his will?" He "sold" them, you say, "to work wickedness," even from their mother's womb. He "gave them up to a reprobate mind," or ever they hung upon their mother's breast. Shall he then condemn them for what they could not help? Shall the Just, the Holy One of Israel, adjudge millions of men to everlasting pain, because their blood moved in their veins? Nay, this they might have helped, by putting an end to their own lives. But could they even thus have escaped from sin? Not without that grace which you suppose God had absolutely determined ever to give them. And yet you suppose him to send them into eternal fire, for not escaping from sin! that is, in plain terms, for not having that grace which God had decreed they should never have! O strange justice! What a picture do you draw of the Judge of all the earth!

32. Are they not rather condemned for not doing good, according to those solemn words of the great Judge, "Depart, ye cursed; for I was an hungered, and ye gave me no meat; I was thirsty, and ye gave me no drink; a stranger, and ye took me not in; I was naked, and ye clothed me not; sick, and in prison, and ye visited me not. Then shall they answer." But how much better an answer do you put into their mouths! Upon your supposition, might they not say, (O consider it well, in meekness and fear!) "Lord, we might have done the outward work; but thou knowest it would have but increased our damnation. We might have fed the hungry, given drink to the thirsty, and covered the naked with a garment. But all these works, without thy special grace, which we never had, nor possibly could have, seeing thou hast eternally decreed to withhold it from us, would only have been splendid sins. They would only have heated the furnace of hell seven times hotter than before." Upon your supposition, might they not say, "Righteous art thou, O Lord; yet let us plead with thee. O, why dost thou condemn us for not doing good? Was it possible for us to do anything well? Did we ever abuse the power of doing good? We never received it, and that thou knowest. Wilt thou, the Holy One, the Just, condemn us for not doing what we never had the power to do? Wilt thou condemn us for not casting down the stars from heaven? for not holding the winds in our fist? Why, it was as possible for us to do this, as to do any work acceptable in thy sight! O Lord, correct us, but with judgment! And, before thou plungest us into everlasting fire, let us know how it was ever possible for us to escape the damnation of hell."

33. Or, how could they have escaped (suppose you assign that; as the cause of their condemnation) from inward sin, from evil desires, from unholy tempers and vile affections? Were they ever able to deliver their own souls, to rescue themselves from this inward hell? If so, their not doing it might justly be laid to their charge, and would leave them without excuse. But it was not so; they never were able to deliver their own sons; they never had the power to rescue themselves from the hands of these bosom enemies. This talent was never put into their hands. How then can they be condemned for hiding it in the earth, for non-improvement of what they never had? Who is able to purify a corrupt heart; to bring a clean thing out of an unclean? Is man, mere man, sufficient for this? No, certainly. God alone. To him only can the polluted of heart say, "Lord, if thou wilt, thou canst make me clean." But what, if he answer, "I will not, because I will not: Be thou unclean still?" Will God doom that man to the bottomless pit, because of that uncleanness which he could not save himself from, and which God could have saved him from, but would not? Verily, were an earthly King to execute such justice as this upon his helpless subjects, it might well be expected that the vengeance of the Lord would soon sweep him from the face of the earth.

34. Perhaps you will say, They are not condemned for actual but for original sin. What do you mean by this term? The inward corruption of our nature? If so, it has been spoken of before. Or do you mean, the sin which Adam committed in paradise? That this is imputed to all men, I allow; yea, that by reason hereof "the whole creation groaneth and travaileth in pain together until now." But that any will be damned for this alone, I allow not, till you show me where it is written. Bring me plain proof from Scripture, and I submit; but till then I utterly deny it.

35. Should you not rather say, that unbelief is the damning sin? and that those who are condemned in that day will be therefore condemned, "because they believed not on the name of the only-begotten Son of God?" But could they believe? Was not this faith both the gift and the work of God in the soul? And was it not a gift which he had eternally decreed never to give them? Was it not a work which he was of old unchangeably determined never to work in their souls? Shall these men be condemned, because God would not work; because they did not receive what God would not give? Could they "ungrasp the hold of his right hand, or force omnipotence?"

36. There is, over and above, a peculiar difficulty here. You say, Christ did not die for these men. But if so, there was an impossibility, in the very nature of the thing, that they should ever savingly believe. For what is

saving faith, but "a confidence in God through Christ, that loved me, and gave himself for me?" Loved thee, thou reprobat! gave himself for thee! Away! thou hast neither part nor lot herein. Thou believe in Christ, thou accursed spirit! damned or ever thou wert born! There never was any object for thy faith; there never was any thing for thee to believe. God himself, (thus must you speak, to be consistent with yourself,) with all his omnipotence, could not make thee believe Christ atoned for thy sins, unless he had made thee believe a lie.

37. If then God be just, there cannot, on your scheme, be any judgment to come. We may add, nor any future state, either of reward or punishment. If there be such a state, God will therein "render to every man according to his works. To them who by patient continuance in well-doing seek for glory and honor and immortality, eternal life; but to them that do not obey the truth, but obey unrighteousness, indignation and wrath, tribulation and anguish upon every soul of man that doeth evil."

But how is this reconcilable with your scheme? You say, The reprobates cannot but do evil; and that the elect, from the day of God's power, cannot but continue in well-doing. You suppose all this is unchangeably decreed; in consequence whereof, God acts irresistibly on the one, and Satan on the other. Then it is impossible for either one or the other to help acting as they do; or rather, to help being acted upon, in the manner wherein they are. For if we speak properly, neither the one nor the other can be said to act at all. Can a stone be said to act, when it is thrown out of a sling? or a ball, when it is projected from a cannon? No more can a man be said to act, if he be only moved by a force he cannot resist. But if the case be thus, you leave no room either for reward or punishment. Shall the stone be rewarded for rising from the sling, or punished for falling down? Shall the cannon-ball be rewarded for flying towards the sun, or punished for receding from it? As incapable of either punishment or reward is the man who is supposed to be impelled by a force he cannot resist. Justice can have no place in rewarding or punishing mere machines, driven to and fro by an external force. So that your supposition of God's ordaining from eternity whatsoever should be done to the end of the world; as well as that of God's acting irresistibly in the elect, and Satan's acting irresistibly in the reprobates; utterly overthrows the Scripture doctrine of rewards and punishments, as well as of a judgment to come.

38. Thus ill does that election which implies reprobation agree with the Scripture account of God's justice. And does it agree any better with his truth? How will you reconcile it with those plain passages? — "Have I any pleasure at all that the wicked should die, saith the Lord God; and not

that he should return from his ways and live? Cast away from you all your transgressions whereby ye have transgressed: For why will ye die, O house of Israel? For I have no pleasure in the death of him that dieth, saith the Lord: Wherefore, turn yourselves, and live ye."(Ezekiel 18:23, etc.) "As I live, saith the Lord God, I have no pleasure in the death of the wicked; but that the wicked turn from his way and live. Turn ye, turn ye from your evil ways: For why will ye die, O house of Israel?" (Ezekiel 33:11.)

39. But perhaps you will say, "These ought to be limited and explained by other passages of Scripture; wherein this doctrine is as clearly affirmed, as it is denied in these." I must answer very plain: If this were true, we must give up all the Scriptures together; nor would the Infidels allow the Bible so honorable a title as that of a "cunningly-devised fable." But it is not true. It has no color of truth. It is absolutely, notoriously false. To tear up the very roots of reprobation, and of all doctrines that have a necessary connection therewith, God declares in his word these three things, and that explicitly, in so many terms:

(1.) "Christ died for all," (2 Corinthians 5:14,) namely, all that were dead in sin, as the words immediately following, fix the sense: Here is the fact affirmed.

(2.) "He is the propitiation for the sins of the whole world," (1 John 2:2,) even of all those for whom he died: Here is the consequence of his dying for all. And,

(3.) "He died for all, that they should not live unto themselves, but unto Him which died for them," (2 Corinthians 5:15,) that they might be saved from their sins: Here is the design, the end of his dying for them.

Now, show me the scriptures wherein God declares in equally express terms,

(1.)"Christ" did not die "for all," but for some only.

(2.)Christ is not "the propitiation for the sins of the whole world;" and,

(3.)"He" did not die "for all," at least, not with that intent, "that they should live unto him who died for them." Show me, I say, the scriptures that affirm these three things in equally express terms. You know there are none. Nor is it possible to evade the force of those above recited, but by supplying in number what is wanting in weight; by heaping abundance of texts together, whereby (though none of them speak home to the point) the patrons of that opinion dazzle the eyes of the unwary, and quite overlay the understanding both of themselves and those that hear them.

40. To proceed: What an account does this doctrine give of the sincerity of God in a thousand declarations, such as these? — "O that there were such an heart in them, that they would fear me, and keep my commandments always, that it might be well with them, and with their children forever!" (Deuteronomy 5:29.) "My people would not hear my voice, and Israel would not obey me. So I gave them up unto their own hearts' lusts, and let them follow their own imaginations. O that my people would have hearkened unto me! For if Israel had walked in my ways, I should soon have put down their enemies, and turned my hand against their adversaries." (Psalm 81:11, etc.) And all this time, you suppose God had unchangeably ordained, that there never should be "such an heart in them!" that it never should be possible for the people whom he thus seemed to lament over, to hearken unto him, or to walk in his ways!

How clear and strong is the reasoning of Dr. Watts on this head! "It is very hard indeed, to vindicate the sincerity of the blessed God or his Son, in their universal offers of grace and salvation to men, and their sending Ministers with such messages and invitations to accept of mercy, if there be not at least a conditional pardon and salvation provided for them.

"His Ministers indeed, as they know not the event of things, may be sincere in offering salvation to all persons, according to their general commission, 'Go ye into all the world, and preach the gospel to every creature.' But how can God or Christ be sincere in sending them with this commission, to offer his grace to all men, if God has not provided such grace for all men, no, not so much as conditionally?

"It is hard to suppose, that the great God, who is truth itself, and faithful in all his dealings, should call upon dying men to trust in a Savior for eternal life, when this Savior has not eternal life intrusted with him to give them if they do as he requires. It is hard to conceive how the great Governor of the world can be sincere in inviting sinners, who are on the brink of hell, to cast themselves upon an empty word of invitation, a mere shadow and appearance of support, if there be nothing real to bear them up from those deeds of destruction, nothing but mere words and empty invitations! Can we think, that the righteous and holy God would encourage his Ministers to call them to leave and rest the weight of their immortal concerns upon a gospel, a covenant of grace, a Mediator, and his merit and righteousness? all which are a mere nothing with regard to them, a heap of empty names, an unsupporting void which cannot uphold them?"

41. Our blessed Lord does indisputably command and invite "all men

everywhere to repent." He calleth all. He sends his ambassadors, in his name, to "preach the gospel to every creature." He himself "preached deliverance to the captives," without any hint of restriction or limitation. But now, in what manner do you represent him, while he is employed in this work? You suppose him to be standing at the prison-doors, having the keys thereof in his hands, and to be continually inviting the prisoners to come forth, commanding them to accept of that invitation, urging every motive which can possibly induce them to, comply with that command; adding the most precious promises, if they obey, the most dreadful threatenings, if they obey not; and all this time you suppose him to be unalterably determined in himself never to open the doors for them! even while he is crying, "Come ye, come ye, from that evil place: For why will ye die, O house of Israel!" "Why!" might one of them reply, "because we cannot help it. We cannot help ourselves; and thou wilt not help us. It is not in our power to break the gates of brass, and it is not thy pleasure to open them. Why will we die! We must die; because it is not thy will to save us." Alas! my brethren, what kind of sincerity is this, which you ascribe to God our Savior?

42. So ill do election and reprobation agree with the truth and sincerity of God! But do they not agree least of all with the scriptural account of his love and goodness? that attribute which God peculiarly claims, wherein he glories above all the rest. It is not written, "God is justice," or "God is truth:" (Although he is just and true in all his ways:) But it is written, "God is love," love in the abstract, without bounds; and "there is no end of his goodness." His love extends even to those who neither love nor fear him. He is good, even to the evil and the unthankful; yea, without any exposition or limitation, to all the children of men. For "the Lord is loving" (or good) "to every man, and his mercy is over all his works."

But how is God good or loving to a reprobate, or one that is not elected? (You may choose either term: For if none but the unconditionally elect are saved, it comes precisely to the same thing.) You cannot say, he is an object of the love or goodness of God, with regard to his eternal state, whom he created, says Mr. Calvin plainly and fairly, in vitae contumeliam et mortis exitium, "to live a reproach, and die everlastingly." Surely, no one can dream, that the goodness of God is at all concerned with this man's eternal state. "However, God is good to him in this world." What! when by reason of God's unchangeable decree, it had been good for this man never to have been born? when his very birth was a curse, not a blessing? "Well, but he now enjoys many of the gifts of God, both gifts of nature and of providence. He has food and raiment, and comforts of various kinds. And are not all these great blessings?" No, not to him. At the price he is to pay for them, every one of these also is a curse. Every one of these comforts is, by an eternal decree, to cost him a thousand pangs in hell. For every moment's pleasure which he now enjoys, he is to suffer the torments of more than a thousand years for the smoke of that pit which is preparing for him ascendeth up for ever and ever. God knew this would be the fruit of whatever he should enjoy, before the vapor of life fled away. He designed it should. It was his very purpose, in giving him those enjoyments. So that, by all these, (according to your account,) he is, in truth and reality, only fatting the ox for the slaughter. "Nay, but God gives him grace too." Yes; but what kind of grace? Saving grace, you own, he has none; none of a saving nature. And the common grace he has was not given with any design to save his soul; nor with any design to do him any good at all; but only to restrain him from hurting the elect. So far from doing him good, that this grace also necessarily increases his damnation. "And God knows this," you say, "and designed it should; it was one great end for which he gave it!" Then I desire to know, how is God good or loving to. this man, either with regard to time or eternity?

43. Let us suppose a particular instance: Here stands a man who is reprobated from all eternity; or, if you would express it more smoothly, one who is not elected, whom God eternally decreed to pass by. Thou hast nothing therefore to expect from God after death, but to be cast into the lake of fire burning with brimstone; God having consigned thy unborn soul to hell, by a decree which cannot pass away. And from the time thou wast born under the irrevocable curse of God, thou canst have no peace. For there is no peace to the wicked; and such thou art doomed to continue, even from thy mother's womb. Accordingly, God giveth thee of this world's goods, on purpose to enhance thy damnation. He giveth thee now substance or friends in order hereafter to heap the more coals of fire upon thy head. He filleth thee with food, he maketh thee fat and well liking, to make thee a more specious sacrifice to his vengeance. Good nature, generosity, a good understanding, various knowledge, it may be, or eloquence, are the flowers wherewith he adorneth thee, thou poor victim, before thou art; brought to the slaughter. Thou hast grace too! but what grace? Not saving grace. That is not for thee, but for the elect only. Thine may properly be termed, damning grace; since it is not only such in the event, but in the intention. Thou receivedst it of God for that very end, that thou mightest receive the greater damnation. It was given, not to convert thee, but only to convince; not to make thee without sin, but without excuse; not to destroy but to arm the worm that never dieth, and

to blow up the fire that never shall be quenched.

44. Now, I beseech you to consider calmly, how is God good or loving to this man? Is not this such love as makes your blood run cold? as causes the ears of him that heareth to tingle? And can you believe there is that man on earth or in hell, who can truly tell God, "Thus hast thou done?" Can you think, that the loving, the merciful God, ever dealt thus with any soul which he hath made? But you must and do believe this, if you believe unconditional election. For it holds reprobation in its bosom; they never were, never can be, divided. Take then your choice. If, for the sake of election, you will swallow reprobation, well. But if you cannot digest this, you must necessarily give up unconditional election.

45. "But you cannot do this; for then you should be called a Pelagian, an Arminian, and what not." And are you afraid of hard names? Then you have not begun to be a disciple of Jesus Christ. No, that is not the case. But you are afraid, if you do not hold election, you must hold free-will, and so rob God of his glory in man's salvation."

I answer,

(1.)Many of the greatest maintainers of election utterly deny the consequence, and do not allow, that even natural free-will in man is repugnant to God's glory. These accordingly assert, that every man living has a measure of natural free-will. So the Assembly of Divines, (and therein the body of Calvinists both in England and Scotland,) "God hath endued the will of man with that natural liberty that is neither forced, nor, by an absolute necessity of nature, determined to do good or evil:" (Chap. 9:) And this they assert of man in his fallen state even before he receives the grace of God.

(2) But I do not carry free-will so far: (I mean, not in moral things:) Natural free-will, in the present state of mankind, I do not understand: I only assert, that there is a measure of free will supernaturally restored to every man, together with that supernatural light which "enlightens every man that cometh into the world." But indeed, whether this be natural or no, as to your objection it matters not. For that equally lies against both, against any free-will of any kind; your assertion being thus, "If man has any free-will, God cannot have the whole glory of his salvation;" or, "It is not so much for the glory of God, to save man as a free agent, put into a capacity of concurring with his grace on the one hand, and of resisting it on the other; as to save him in the way of a necessary agent, by a power which he cannot possibly resist."

46. With regard to the former of these assertions, "If man has any free-will, then God cannot have the whole glory of his salvation," is your meaning this: "If man has any power to 'work out his own salvation,' then God cannot have the whole glory?" If it be, I must ask again, What do you mean by God's "having the whole glory?" Do you mean, "His doing the whole work, without any concurrence on man's part?" If so, your assertion is, "If man do at all 'work together with God,' in 'working out his own salvation,' then God does not do the whole work, without man's 'working together with Him.'" Most true, most sure: But cannot you see, how God nevertheless may have all the glory? Why, the very power to "work together with Him" was from God. Therefore to Him is all the glory. Has not even experience taught you this? Have you not often felt, in a particular temptation, power either to resist or yield to the grace of God? And when you have yielded to "work together with Him," did you not find it very possible, notwithstanding, to give him all the glory? So that both experience and Scripture are against you here, and make it clear to every impartial inquirer, that though man has freedom to work or not "work together with God," yet may God have the whole glory of his salvation.

47. If then you say, "We ascribe to God alone the whole glory of our salvation;" I answer, So do we too. If you add, "Nay, but we affirm, that God alone does the whole work, without man's working at all;" in one sense, we allow this also. We allow, it is the work of God alone to justify, to sanctify, and to glorify; which three comprehend the whole of salvation. Yet we cannot allow, that man can only resist, and not in any wise "work together with God;" or that God is so the whole worker of our salvation, as to exclude man's working at all. This I dare not say; for I cannot prove it by Scripture; nay, it is flatly contrary thereto; for the Scripture is express, that (having received power from God) we are to "work out our own salvation;" and that (after the work of God is begun in our souls) we are "workers together with Him."

48. Your objection, proposed in another form, is this: "It is not so much for the glory of God, to save man as a free agent, I put into a capacity of either concurring with, or resisting, his grace; as to save him in the way of a necessary agent, by a power which he cannot possibly resist."
O that the Lord would answer for himself! that he would arise and maintain his own cause! that he would no longer suffer his servants, few as they are, to weaken one another's hands, and to be wearied not only with the "contradiction of sinners," but even of those who are in a measure saved from sin! "Woe is me, that I am constrained to dwell with Meshech!

among them that are enemies to peace! I labor for peace; but when I speak thereof, they still make themselves ready for battle."

49. If it must be, then, let us look one another in the face. How is it more for the glory of God to save man irresistibly, than to save him as a free agent, by such grace as he may either concur with or resist? I fear you have a confused, unscriptural notion of "the glory of God." What do you mean by that expression? The glory of God, strictly speaking, is his glorious essence and his attributes, which have been ever of old. And this glory admits of no increase, being the same yesterday, today, and forever. But the Scripture frequently speaks of the glory of God, in a sense something different from this; meaning thereby, the manifestation of his essential glory, of his eternal power and godhead, and of his glorious attributes, more especially his justice, mercy, and truth. And it is in this sense alone that the glory of God is said to be advanced by man. Now then, this is the point which it lies on you to prove: "That it does more eminently manifest the glorious attributes of God, more especially his justice, mercy, and truth, to save man irresistibly, than to save him by such grace as it is in his power either to concur with, or to resist."

50. But you must not imagine I will be so unwise as to engage you here on this single point. I shall not now dispute (which yet might be done,) whether salvation by irresistible grace, (which indeed makes man a mere machine, and, consequently, no more rewardable and punishable,) whether, I say, salvation by irresistible grace, considered apart from its consequences, manifest the glory of God more or less than salvation by grace which may be resisted. Not so; but, by the assistance of God, I shall take your whole scheme together; irresistible grace for the elect, implying the denial of saving grace to all others; or unconditional election with its inseparable companion, unconditional reprobation.

The case is clearly this: You may drive me, on the one hand, unless I will contradict myself, or retract my principles, to own a measure of free-will in every man; (though not by nature, as the Assembly of Divines;) and, on the other hand, I can drive you, and every assertor of unconditional election, unless you will contradict yourself, or retract your principles, to own unconditional reprobation.

Stand forth, then, free-will on the one side, and reprobation on the other; and let us see whether the one scheme, attended with the absurdity, as you think it, of free-will, or the other scheme, attended with the absurdity of reprobation, be the more defensible. Let us see (if it please the Father of Lights to open the eyes of our understanding) which of these is more for the glory of God, for the display of his glorious attributes, for the manifestation of his wisdom, justice, and mercy, to the sons of men.

51. First, his wisdom. If man be in some measure free; if, by that light which "lighteneth every man that comes into the world," there be "set before him life and death, good and evil;" then how gloriously does the manifold wisdom of God appear in the whole economy of man's salvation! Being willing that all men should be saved, yet not willing to force them thereto; willing that men should be saved, yet not as trees or stones, but as men, as reasonable creatures, endued with understanding to discern what is good, and liberty either to accept or refuse it; how does he suit the whole scheme of his dispensations to this his proqesiv, his plan, "the counsel of his will!" His first step is to enlighten the understanding by that general knowledge of good and evil. To this he adds many secret reproofs, if they act contrary to this light; many inward convictions, which there is not a man on earth who has not often felt. At other times he gently moves their wills, he draws and woos them, as it were, to walk in the light. He instills into their hearts good desires, though perhaps they know not from whence they come. Thus far he proceeds with all the children of men, yea, even with those who have not the knowledge of his written word. But in this, what a field of wisdom is displayed, suppose man to be in some degree a free agent! How is every part of it suited to this end! to save man, as man; to set life and death before him, and then persuade (not force) him to choose life. According to this grand purpose of God, a perfect rule is first set before him, to serve as a "lantern to his feet, and a light in all his paths." This is offered to him in a form of a law, enforced with the strongest sanctions, the most glorious rewards for them that obey, the severest penalties on them that break it. To reclaim these, God uses all manner of ways; he tries every avenue of their souls. He applies sometimes to their understanding, showing them the folly of their sins; sometimes to their affections, tenderly expostulating with them for their ingratitude, and even condescending to ask, "What could I have done for" you (consistent with my eternal purpose, not to force you) "which I have not done?" He intermixes sometimes threats, — "Except ye repent, ye shall all likewise perish;" sometimes promises, — "Your sins and your iniquities will I remember no more." Now, what wisdom is seen in all this, if man may indeed choose life or death! But if every man be unalterably consigned to heaven or hell before he comes from his mother's womb, where is the wisdom of this; of dealing with him, in every respect, as if he were free, when it is no such thing? What avails, what can this whole dispensation of God avail a reprobate? What are promises or threats, expostulations or reproofs to thee, thou firebrand of hell? What, indeed,

(O my brethren, suffer me to speak, for I am full of matter!) but empty farce, but mere grimace, sounding words, that mean just nothing? O where (to wave all other considerations now) is the wisdom of this proceeding! To what end does all this apparatus serve? If you say, "To insure his damnation;" alas, what needeth that, seeing this was insured before the foundation of the world! Let all mankind then judge, which of these accounts is more for the glory of God's wisdom!

52. We come next to his justice. Now, if man be capable of choosing good or evil, then he is a proper object of the justice of God, acquitting or condemning, rewarding or punishing. But otherwise he is not. A mere machine is not capable of being either acquitted or condemned. Justice cannot punish a stone for falling to the ground; nor, on your scheme, a man for falling into sin. For he can no more help it than the stone, if he be, in your sense, fore-ordained to this condemnation. Why does this man sin? "He cannot cease from sin." Why cannot he cease from sin? "Because he has no saving grace." Why has he no saving grace? "Because God, of his own good pleasure, hath eternally decreed not to give it him." Is he then under an unavoidable necessity of sinning? "Yes, as much as a stone is of falling. He never had any more power to cease from evil, than a stone has to hang in the air." And shall this man, for not doing what he never could do, and for doing what he never could avoid, be sentenced to depart into everlasting fire, prepared for the devil and his angels? "Yes, because it is the sovereign will of God." Then "you have either found a new God, or made one!" This is not the God of the Christians. Our God is just in all his ways; he reapeth not where he hath not strewed. He requireth only according to what he hath given; and where he hath given little, little is required. The glory of his justice is this, to "reward every man according to his works." Hereby is that glorious attribute shown, evidently set forth before men and angels, in that it is accepted of every man according to that he hath, and not according to that he hath not. This is that just decree which cannot pass, either in time or in eternity.

Thus one scheme gives the justice of God its full scope, leaves room for it to be largely displayed in all its branches; whereas the other makes it a mere shadow; yea, brings it absolutely to nothing.

53. Just as gloriously does it display his love; supposing it to be fixed on one in ten of his creatures, (might I not rather say, on one in a hundred?) and to have no regard to the rest. Let the ninety-and-nine reprobates perish without mercy. It is enough for him, to love and save the one elect. But why will he have mercy on these alone, and leave all those to inevitable destruction? "He will — because he will!" O that God would

give unto you who thus speak, meekness of wisdom! Then, would I ask, What would the universal voice of mankind pronounce of the man that should act thus? that being able to deliver millions of men from death with a single breath of his mouth, should refuse to save any more than one in a hundred, and say, "I will not, because I will not!" How then do you exalt the mercy of God, when you ascribe such a proceeding to him? What a strange comment is this on his own word, that "his mercy is over all his works!"

Do you think to evade this by saying, "His mercy is more displayed, in irresistibly saving the elect, than it would be in giving the choice of salvation to all men, and actual salvation to those that accepted it?" How so? Make this appear if you can. What proof do you bring of this assertion? I appeal to every impartial mind, whether the reverse be not obviously true; whether the mercy of God would not be far less gloriously displayed, in saving a few by his irresistible power, and leaving all the rest without help, without hope, to perish everlastingly, than in offering salvation to every creature, actually saving all that consent thereto, and doing for the rest all that infinite wisdom, almighty power, and boundless love can do, without forcing them to be saved, which would be to destroy the very nature that he had given them. I appeal, I say, to every impartial mind, and to your own, if not quite blinded with prejudice, which of these accounts places the mercy of God in the most advantageous light.

54. Perhaps you will say, "But there are other attributes of God, namely, his sovereignty, unchangeableness, and faithfulness. I hope you do not deny these." I answer, No; by no means. The sovereignty of God appears,

(1.)In fixing from eternity that decree touching the sons of men, "He that believeth shall be saved: He that believeth not shall be damned."

(2.)In all the general circumstances of creation; in the time, the place, the manner of creating all things; in appointing the number and kinds of creatures, visible and invisible.

(3.)In allotting the natural endowments of men, these to one, and those to another.

(4.)In disposing the time, place, and other outward circumstances (as parents, relations) attending the: birth of every one.

(5.)In dispensing the various gifts of his Spirit, for the edification of his Church.

(6.)In ordering all temporal things, as health, fortune, friends, everything short of eternity.

But in disposing the eternal states of men, (allowing only what was observed under the first article,) it is clear, that not sovereignty alone, but justice, mercy, and truth hold the reins. The Governor of heaven and earth, the I AM, over all, God blessed forever, takes no step here but as these direct, and prepare the way before his face. This is his eternal and irresistible will, as he hath revealed unto us by his Spirit; declaring in the strongest terms, adding his oath to his word, and, because he would swear by no greater, swearing by himself, "As I live, saith the Lord God, I have no pleasure in the death of him that dieth." The death of him that dieth can never be resolved into my pleasure or sovereign will. No; it is impossible. We challenge all mankind, to bring on clear, scriptural proof to the contrary. You can bring no scripture proof that God ever did, or assertion that he ever will, act as mere sovereign in eternally condemning any soul that ever was or will be born into the world.

55. Now, you are probably thinking of Esau and Pharaoh. Do you then set it down as an unquestionable truth, that these were eternally condemned by the mere sovereign will of God? Are you sure that they were eternally condemned? Even that point is not altogether certain. It is nowhere asserted in holy writ; and it would cost you some pains to prove it. It is true, Pharaoh's death was a punishment from God; but it does not follow, that he was punished everlastingly. And if he was, it was not by the mere sovereign will of God, but because of his own stubbornness and impenitence.

Of this Moses has given us a particular account: Accordingly we read, "When Pharaoh saw that there was respite," (after he was delivered from the plague of frogs,) "he hardened his heart, and hearkened not unto them." (Exodus 8:15.) So after the plague of flies, "Pharaoh hardened his heart at this time also, neither would he let the people go." (Verse 32.) Again: "When Pharaoh saw that the rain and the hail were ceased, he sinned yet more, and hardened his heart, he and his servants." (9:34.) After God had given him all this space to repent, and had expostulated with him for his obstinate impenitence, in those solemn words, "How long wilt thou refuse to humble thyself before me?" (10:3;) what wonder is it, if God then "hardened his heart," that is, permitted Satan to harden it? if he at length wholly withdrew his softening grace, and "gave him up to a reprobate mind?"

56. The case of Esau is widely different from this; although his conduct also is blamable in many points. The first was, the selling his birth-right to Jacob. (Genesis 25:31, etc.) The next, his marrying against his father's consent. (26:34, 35.) But it is highly probable he was sensible of his fault; because Isaac appears to have been fully reconciled to him when he said,

"My son, make me savory meat, that my soul may bless thee before I die." (27:4.)

In the following verses we have an account of the manner wherein he was supplanted by his brother Jacob. Upon Isaac's relation of this, "Esau cried with a great and exceeding bitter cry, and said unto his father, Bless me, even me also, O my father!" (Verse 34.) But "he found no place," says the Apostle, "for repentance," for recovering the blessing, "though he sought it carefully with tears." "Thy brother," said Isaac, "hath taken away thy blessing: I have blessed him, yell, and he shall be blessed." So that all Esau's sorrow and tears could not recover his birth-right, and the blessing annexed thereto.

And yet there is great reason to hope, that Esau (as well as Jacob) is now in Abraham's bosom. For although for a time "he hated Jacob," and afterward came against him "with four hundred men," very probably designing to take revenge for the injuries he had sustained; yet we and, when they met, "Esau ran and embraced him, and fell on his neck and kissed him." So thoroughly had God changed his heart! And why should we doubt but that happy change continued?

57. You can ground no solid objection to this on St. Paul's words in the Epistle to the Romans: "It was said unto her, The elder shall serve the younger. As it is written, Jacob have I loved, but Esau have I hated." (9:12, 13.) For it is undeniably plain, that both these scriptures relate, not to the persons of Jacob and Esau, but to their descendants; the Israelites sprung from Jacob, and the Edomites sprung from Esau. In this sense only did "the elder" (Esau) "serve the younger;" not in his person, (for Esau never served Jacob,) but in his posterity. The posterity of the elder brother served the posterity of the younger.

The other text referred to by the Apostle runs thus: "I loved Jacob, and I hated Esau, and laid his mountains and his heritage waste for the dragons of the wilderness." (Malachi 1:2, 3.) Whose heritage was it that God laid waste? Not that which Esau personally enjoyed; but that of his posterity, the Edomites, for their enormous sins, largely described by several of the Prophets. So neither here is there any instance of any man being finally condemned by the mere sovereign will of God.

58. The unchangeableness of God, we allow likewise. "In him is no variable less, neither shadow of turning." But you seem to lie under a mistake concerning this also, for want of observing the scripture account of it. The Scripture teaches,

(1) That God is unchangeable with regard to his decrees. But what decrees? The same that he has commanded to be preached to every

creature: "He that believeth shall be saved; he that believeth not shall be damned." The Scripture teaches,

(2.) That God is unchangeable with regard to his love and hatred. But how? Observe this well; for it is your grand mistake, and the root of almost all the rest. God unchangeably loveth righteousness, and hateth iniquity. Unchangeably he loveth faith, and unchangeably hateth unbelief. In consequence hereof he unchangeably loves the righteous, and hateth the workers of iniquity. He unchangeably loves them that believe, and hates willful, obstinate unbelievers.

So that the scripture account of God's unchangeableness with regard to his decrees, is this: He has unchangeably decreed to save holy believers, and to condemn obstinate, impenitent unbelievers. And according to Scripture, his unchangeableness of affection properly and primarily regards tempers and not persons; and persons (as Enoch, Noah, Abraham) only as those tempers are found in them. Let then the unchangeableness of God be put upon the right foot; let the Scripture be allowed to fix the objects of it, and it will as soon prove transubstantiation, as unconditional election.

59. The faithfulness of God may be termed a branch of his truth. He will perform what he hath promised. But then let us inquire of the oracles of God, To whom are the promises made? the promises of life and immortality? The answer is, "To Abraham and his seed;" that is, to those who "walk in the steps of that faith of their father Abraham." To those who believe, as believers, are the gospel promises made. To these hath the faithful God engaged, that he will do what he hath spoken. "He will fulfill his covenant and promise which he hath made to a thousand generations:" The sum of which is, (as we find it expressly declared by the Spirit of God,) "The Lord will give grace" (more grace) "and glory; and no good thing will he withhold from them that live a godly life."

60. This covenant of God I understand; but I have heard of another which I understand not. I have heard, "that God the Father made a covenant with his Son, before the world began, wherein the Son agreed to suffer such and such things, and the Father to give him such and such souls for a recompence; that in consequence of this, those souls must be saved, all those only, so that all others must be damned." I beseech you, where is this written? In what part of Scripture is this covenant to be found? We may well expect a thing of this moment to be revealed very expressly, with the utmost clearness and solemnity. But where is this done? And if it is not done, if there is no such account in all the Bible; which shall we wonder at most, that any serious man should advance, or that thousands should believe, so strange an assertion, without one plain text of Scripture

to support it, from Genesis to the Revelation?

61. I suppose you do not imagine that the bare word covenant, if it occurred ever so often in holy writ, is a proof of any such covenant as this. The grand covenant which we allow to be mentioned therein, is a covenant between God and man, established in the hands of a Mediator, "who tasted death for every man," and thereby purchased it for all the children of men. The tenor of it (so often mentioned already) is this: "Whosoever believeth unto the end, so as to show his faith by his works, I the Lord will reward that soul eternally. But whosoever will not believe, and consequently dieth in his sins, I will punish him with everlasting destruction."

62. To examine thoroughly whether this covenant between God and man be unconditional or conditional, it may be needful to go back as far as Abraham, the father of the faithful; to inquire what manner of covenant it was which God made with him; and whether any reason be assigned of God's peculiarly blessing Abraham, and all the nations of the earth in him. The first mention of the covenant between God and him, occurs Genesis 15:18: "The same day the Lord made a covenant with Abram, saying, Unto thy seed will I give this land." But this is much more explicitly related in chapter 17:1, etc.: "The Lord appeared unto Abram, and said unto him, I am the almighty God; walk before me, and be thou perfect. And I will make my covenant between me and thee, and will multiply thee exceedingly. And Abram fell on his face: And God talked with him, saying, As for me, behold, my covenant is with thee, and thou shalt be a father of many nations. Neither shall thy name any more be called Abram, but thy name shall be Abraham; for a father of many nations have I made thee. And I will establish my covenant between me and thee, and thy seed after thee, for an everlasting covenant, to be a God unto thee, and to thy seed after thee. Every man-child among you shall be circumcised; — it shall be a token of the covenant betwixt me and you. The uncircumcised man-child shall be cut off; he hath broken my covenant." So we see, this original covenant, though everlasting, was conditional, and man's failing in the condition cleared God.

63. We have St. Paul's account of this covenant of God with Abraham, in the fourth chapter of his Epistle to the Romans, verse 3, etc.: "Abraham," saith he, "believed God, and it was counted to him for righteousness." (This was a little before God established his covenant with him, and is related Genesis 15:6.) "And he received the sign of circumcision, a seal of the righteousness of the faith which he had yet being uncircumcised, that he might as the father of all them that believe, though they be not

circumcised, that righteousness might be imputed unto them also; and the father of circumcision" (that is, of them that are circumcised) "to them who are not of the circumcision only, but also walk in the steps of that faith of our father Abraham, which he had being yet uncircumcised." Now, if these words do not express a conditional covenant, certainly none can.

64. The nature and ground of this covenant of God with Abraham is farther explained: "And the Lord said, Shall I hide from Abraham that thing which I do, seeing all the nations of the earth shall be blessed in him? For I know him, that he will command his children, and his household after him: And they shall keep the way of the Lord, to do justice and judgment; that the Lord may bring unto Abraham that which he hath spoken of him." (Genesis 18:17, etc.)

Does God say here, "I will do it, because I will" Nothing less. The reason is explicitly assigned: "All nations shall be blessed in him; for he will command his children, and they shall keep the way of the Lord."

The reason is yet more (clearly it cannot, but more) fully set down in the twenty-second chapter, verse 16, etc.: "By myself have I sworn, saith the Lord, because thou hast done this thing, and hast not withheld thy son, thine only son: That in blessing "will bless thee; and in thy seed shall all the nations of the earth be blessed;" that is, the Messiah shall spring from thee, "because thou hast obeyed my voice."

This is yet again declared: "And the Lord appeared unto Isaac, and said, — Sojourn in this land, and I will be with thee, and bless thee: For unto thee, and unto thy seed, I will perform the oath which I swear unto Abraham thy father. In thy seed shall all nations of the earth be blessed: Because that Abraham obeyed my voice, and kept my charge, my commandments, my statutes, and my laws." (Genesis 26:2, etc.)

65. This covenant, made to Abraham and his seed, is mentioned again: "And the Lord called unto Moses, saying, Thus shalt thou say to the house of Jacob, and tell the children of Israel: Ye have seen what I did to the Egyptians, and how I bare you on eagles' wings, and brought you unto myself. Now therefore, if ye will obey my voice indeed, and keep my covenant, then ye shall be a peculiar treasure unto me above all people." (Exodus 19:3, etc.)

In the following chapter, God declares the terms of the covenant they were to keep, in ten commandments. And these themselves are sometimes termed "the covenant," sometimes "the book of the covenant." So, after God had made an end of speaking to the people, it is said, "And Moses wrote all the words of the Lord, and rose up early in the morning, — and he took the book of the covenant, and read in the audience of the people;

and they said, All that the Lord hath said will we do. And Moses took the blood," (of the burnt-offering,) "and sprinkled it on the people, and said, Behold the blood of the covenant, which the Lord hath made with you concerning all these words." (24:4, etc.)

After the people had broken this covenant by worshipping the golden calf, God renews it, Exodus 34, where we read, "And the Lord said unto Moses, Write thou these words: For after the tenor of these words I have made a covenant with thee and with Israel — and he wrote upon the tables the words of the covenant, the ten commandments." (Verses 27, 28.)

66. According to the tenor of this covenant, made to Abraham and his seed, God afterward declares, "If ye walk in my statutes, and keep my commandments, and do them; then I will establish my covenant with you, and I will be your God, and ye shall be my people. But if ye will not hearken, unto me, so that ye will not do all my commandments, but that ye break my covenant; I will set my face against you, and I will avenge the quarrel of my covenant. Yet if they shall confess their iniquity, and if their uncircumcised hearts be humbled; then will I remember my covenant with Jacob, and also my covenant with Isaac, and also my covenant with Abraham will I remember." (Leviticus 26:3, etc.) Consequently the covenant with Abraham, Isaac, and Jacob, was conditional, as well as that with their posterity.

67. "But is not the faithfulness of God engaged to keep all that now believe from falling away?" I cannot say that. Whatever assurance God may give to particular souls, I find no general promise in holy writ, "that none who once believes shall finally fall." Yet, to say the truth, this is so pleasing an opinion, so agreeable to flesh and blood, so suitable to whatever of nature remains in those who have tasted the grace of God, that I see nothing but the mighty power of God which can restrain any who hears it from closing with it. But still it wants one thing to recommend it, — plain, cogent scripture proof.

Arguments from experience alone will never determine this point. They can only prove thus much, on the one hand, that our Lord is exceeding patient; that he is peculiarly unwilling any believer should perish; that he bears long, very long, with all their follies, waiting to be gracious, and to heal their backsliding; and that he does actually bring back many lost sheep, who, to man's apprehensions, were irrecoverable: But all this does not amount to a convincing proof, that no believer can or does fall from grace. So that this argument, from experience, will weigh little with those who believe the possibility of falling.

And it will weigh full as little with those who do not; for if you produce ever so many examples of those who were once strong in faith, and are now more abandoned than ever, they will evade it by saying, "O, but they will be brought back; they will not die in their sins." And if they do die in their sins, we come no nearer; we have not gained one point still: For it is easy to say, "They were only hypocrites; they never had true faith." Therefore Scripture alone can determine this question; and Scripture does so fully determine it, that there needs only to set down a very few texts, with some short reflections upon them.

68. That one who is a true believer, or, in other words, one who is holy or righteous in the judgment of God himself, may nevertheless finally fall from grace, appears,

(1.) From the word of God by Ezekiel: "When the righteous turneth away from his righteousness, and committeth iniquity: In his trespass that he hath trespassed, and in his sin that he hath sinned, in them shall he die." (18:24.)

Do you object, "This chapter relates wholly and solely to the Jewish Church and nation?" 32 I answer, Prove this. Till then, I shall believe that many parts of it concern all mankind.

If you say,

(2.)"The righteousness spoken of in this chapter was merely an outward righteousness, without an inward principle of grace or holiness:" I ask, How is this consistent with the thirty-first verse: "Cast away from you all your transgressions whereby ye have transgressed; and make you a new heart and a new spirit?" Is this a "merely outward righteousness, without any inward principle of grace or holiness?"

69. Will you add, "But admitting the person here spoken of to be a truly righteous man, what is here said is only a supposition?" That I flatly deny. Read over the chapter again; and you will see the facts there laid down to be not barely supposed, but expressly asserted.

That the death here mentioned is eternal death, appears from the twenty-sixth verse: "When a righteous man turneth away from his righteousness, and committeth iniquity, and dieth in them," — here is temporal death; "for his iniquity that he hath done he shall die." Here is death eternal.

If you assert, "Both these expressions signify the same thing, and not two different deaths," you put a palpable force upon the text, in order to make the Holy Ghost speak nonsense.

"'Dying in his iniquity,'" you say, "is the same thing as 'dying for his iniquity.'" Then the text means thus: "When he dieth in them, he shall die in them." A very deep discovery!

But you say, "It cannot be understood of eternal death; because they might be delivered from it by repentance and reformation." And why might they not by such repentance as is mentioned in the thirty-first verse be delivered from eternal death?

"But the whole chapter," you think, "has nothing to do with the spiritual and eternal affairs of men."

I believe every impartial man will think quite the contrary, if he reads calmly either the beginning of it, — "All souls are mine, saith the Lord God; the soul that sinneth, it shall die;" where I can by no means allow that by the death of the soul is meant only a temporal affliction; or the conclusion, — "Repent, and turn yourselves from all your transgressions; so iniquity shall not be your ruin. Cast away from you all your transgressions, whereby ye have transgressed, and make you a new heart, and a new spirit: For why will ye die, O house of Israel?"

It remains then, one who is righteous in the judgment of God himself, may finally fall from grace.

70. Secondly. That one who is ended with the faith which produces a good conscience, may nevertheless finally fall, appears from the words of St. Paul to Timothy: "War a good warfare; holding faith and a good conscience; which some having put away concerning faith have made shipwreck." (1 Timothy 1:18, 19.)

Observe,

(1.)These men had once the faith that produces "a good conscience;" which they once had, or they could not have "put it away."

(2.)They made shipwreck of the faith, which necessarily implies the total and final loss of it.

You object: "Nay, the putting away a good conscience does not suppose they had it, but rather that they had it not."

This is really surprising. But how do you prove it? "Why, by Acts 13:46, where St. Paul says to the Jews, 'It was necessary that the word of God should first have been spoken to you: But seeing ye put it from you, lo, we turn to the Gentiles.' Here you see the Jews, who never had the gospel, are said to put it away."

How! Are you sure they "never had what they are here said to put away?" Not so: What they put away, it is undeniable, they had, till they put it away; namely, "the word of God spoken" by Paul and Barnabas. This instance, therefore, makes full against you. It proves just the reverse of what you cited it for.

But you object further: "Men may have a good conscience, in some sense, without true faith."

I grant it, in a restrained, limited sense; but not a good conscience, simply and absolutely speaking. But such is that of which the Apostle here speaks, and which he exhorts Timothy to "hold fast." Unless you apprehend that the holding it fast likewise "rather supposes he never had it."

"But the faith here mentioned means only the doctrine of faith." I want better proof of this.

It remains, then, one who has the faith which produces a good conscience may yet finally fall.

71. Thirdly. Those who are grafted into the good olive tree, the spiritual, invisible Church, may nevertheless finally fall.

For thus saith the Apostle: "Some of the branches are broken off, and thou art grafted in among them, and with them partakest of the root and fatness of the olive tree. Be not high-minded, but fear: If God spared not the natural branches, take heed lest he spare not thee. Behold the goodness and severity of God! On them which fell, severity; but toward thee, goodness, if thou continue in his goodness: Otherwise thou shalt be cut off." (Romans 11:17, etc.)

We may observe here,

(1.)The persons spoken to were actually ingrafted into the olive tree.

(2.)This olive tree is not barely the outward, visible Church, but the invisible, consisting of holy believers. So the text: "If the first fruit be holy, the lump is holy; and if the root be holy, so are the branches." And "because of unbelief they were broken off, and thou standest by faith."

(3.)Those holy believers were still liable to be cut off from the invisible Church, into which they were then grafted.

(4.)Here is not the least intimation of their being ever grafted in again.

To this you object,

(1.)"This olive tree is not the invisible Church, but only the outward gospel Church state." You affirm this; and I prove the contrary; namely, that it is the invisible Church; for it "consists of holy believers," which none but the invisible Church does.

(2.)"The Jews who were broken off were never true believers in Christ."

I am not speaking of the Jews, but of those Gentiles who are mentioned in the twenty-second verse; whom St. Paul exhorts to "continue in his goodness;" otherwise, saith he, "thou shalt be cut off." Now, I presume these were true believers in Christ. Yet they were still liable to be cut off.

You assert,

(3.)"This is only a cutting off from the outward Church state." But how is this proved? So forced and unnatural a construction requires some argument to support it.

(4.)"There is a strong intimation that they shall be grafted in again." No; not that those Gentiles who did not continue in his goodness should be grafted in after they were once cut off. I cannot find the least intimation of this. "But all Israel shall be saved." I believe they will; but this does not imply the re-ingrafting of these Gentiles.

It remains, then, that those who are grafted into the spiritual, invisible Church, may nevertheless finally fall.

72. Fourthly. Those who are branches of Christ, the true vine, may yet finally fall from grace.

For thus saith our blessed Lord himself: "I am the true vine, and my Father is the husbandman. Every branch in me that beareth not fruit, he taketh away. I am the vine, ye are the branches. If a man abide not in me, he is cast forth as a branch, and is withered; and men gather them, and cast them into the fire, and they are burned." (John 15:1, etc.)

Here we may observe,

(1.)The persons spoken of were in Christ, branches of the true vine.

(2.)Some of these branches abide not in Christ, but "the Father taketh them away."

(3.)The branches which "abide not" are "cast forth," cast out from Christ and his Church.

(4.)They are not only "cast forth," but "withered," consequently, never grafted in again.

(5.)They are not only "cast forth and withered," but also "cast into the fire." And,

(6.)"They are burned." It is not possible for words more strongly to declare that those who are branches of the true vine may finally fall.

"But this," you say, "furnishes an argument for, not against, the persevering of the saints."

Yes, just such an argument for final perseverance, as the above cited words of St. Paul to Timothy.

But how do you make it out? "Why thus: There are two sorts of branches in Christ the vine; the one fruitful, the other unfruitful. The one are eternally chosen; and these abide in him, and can never withdraw away."

Nay, this is the very point to be proved. So that you now immediately and directly beg the question.

"The other sort of branches are such as are in Christ only by profession; who get into Churches, and so are reckoned in Christ; and these in time wither away. These never had any life, grace, or fruitfulness from him." Surely you do not offer this by way of argument! You are again taking for granted the very point to be proved.

But you will prove that "those are branches in Christ, who never had any life or grace from him, because the Churches of Judea and Thessalonica are said to be in Christ, though every individual member was not savingly in him." I deny the consequence; which can never be made good, unless you can prove that those very Jews or Thessalonians who never had any life or grace from him are nevertheless said by our Lord to be "branches in him." It remains, that true believers, who are branches of the true vine, may nevertheless finally fall.

73. Fifthly. Those who so effectually know Christ, as by that knowledge to have escaped the pollutions of the world, may yet fall back into those pollutions, and perish everlastingly.

For thus saith the Apostle Peter, "If, after they have escaped the pollutions of the world, through the knowledge of the Lord and Savior Jesus Christ," (the only possible way of escaping them,) "they are entangled again therein and overcome, the latter end is worse with them than the beginning." (2 Peter 2:20.)

But you say,

(1.) "Their knowledge was not an experimental knowledge." And how do you prove this? "Because had it been such, they could not have lost it." You are begging the question again.

(2.) "Escaping the pollutions of the world signifies no more than an outward reformation." How prove you that? You aim at no proof at all. But he that will grant it, may.

(3.) "These persons never had any change wrought upon them. They were no other than dogs and swine, not only before and after, but even while they outwardly abstained from gross enormities."

I grant, that before and after that time, during which they "escaped the pollutions of the world," (or, as St. Peter words it in his former Epistle, "the corruption that is in the world,") they might well be termed either "dogs" or "swine," for their gross enormities. But that they deserved such an appellation during that time, I cannot grant without some proof.

It remains, that those who, by the inward knowledge of Christ, have escaped the pollutions of the world may yet fall back into those pollutions, and perish everlastingly.

74. Sixthly. Those who see the light of the glory of God in the face of Jesus Christ, and who have been made partakers of the Holy Ghost, of the witness and the fruits of the Spirit, may nevertheless so fall from God as to perish everlastingly.

For thus saith the writer to the Hebrews: "It is impossible for those who were once enlightened, and have tasted of the heavenly gift, and were made partakers of the Holy Ghost, if they fall away, to renew them again to repentance; seeing they crucify to themselves the Son of God afresh, and put him to an open shame." (6:4-6.)

Must not every unprejudiced person see, the expressions here used are so strong and clear, that they cannot, without gross and palpable wresting, be understood of any but true believers?

"But the Apostle makes only a supposition, 'If they shall fall away."

The Apostle makes no supposition at all. There is no if in the original. The words are, Adunaton touv apax fwtisqentav — kai parapesontav; that is, in plain English, "It is impossible to renew again unto repentance those who were once enlightened and have fallen away."

"No. The words in the original lie literally thus: 'It is impossible for those who were once enlightened, and they falling away, to renew them again unto repentance;' that is, should they fall away, which is, in plain English, if they fall away."

Excuse me for speaking plain English here. "Shall a man lie for God?" Either you or I do; for I flatly aver, (and let all that understand Greek judge between us,) that the words in the original do not lie literally thus, "and they falling away;" (if so, they must be kai parapiptontav, in the present tense; not kai parapesontav, in the indefinite;) but that they are translated, "and have fallen away," as literally as the English tongue will bear.

Therefore here is no if in the case, no supposition at all, but a plain declaration of matter of fact.

75. "But why do you imagine these persons were true believers?" Because all the expressions, in their easy, natural sense, imply it.

They "were once enlightened;" an expression familiar with the Apostle, and never by him applied to any but believers. So "the God of our Lord Jesus Christ give unto you the Spirit of wisdom and revelation: The eyes of your understanding being enlightened, that ye may know what is the hope of his calling; and what is the exceeding greatness of his power to us-ward that believe." (Ephesians 1:17, etc.) So again: "God, who commanded The light to shine out of darkness, hath shined in our hearts, to give the light of the knowledge of the glory of God in the face of Jesus

Christ." (2 Corinthians 4:6.)

"Nay, 'they were enlightened' means only, they were baptized, or knew the doctrines of the gospel."

I cannot believe this, till you bring me a few passages from St. Paul's writings, wherein that expression is evidently taken in either of these senses.

Again: They "had tasted of the heavenly gift," (emphatically so called,) "and were made partakers of the Holy Ghost." So St. Peter likewise couples them together: "Be baptized for the remission of sins, and ye shall receive the gift of the Holy Ghost;" (Acts 2:38;) whereby the love of God was shed abroad in their hearts, with all the other fruits of the Spirit.

The expression, "They had tasted of the heavenly gift," is taken from the Psalmist, "Taste and see that the Lord is good." As if he had said, Be ye as assured of his love, as of anything you see with your eyes. And let the assurance thereof be sweet to your soul, as honey is to your tongue.

"But this means only, they had some notions of remission of sins and heaven, and some desires after them; and they had received the extraordinary gifts of the Holy Ghost." This you affirm; but without any color of proof.

It remains, that those who see the light of the glory of God in the face of Jesus Christ, and who have been made partakers of the Holy Ghost, of the witness and the fruits of the Spirit, may nevertheless so fall from God as to perish everlastingly.

76. Seventhly. Those who live by faith may yet fall from God, and perish everlastingly.

For thus saith the Apostle: "The just shall live by faith: But if any man draw back, my soul shall have no pleasure in him." (Hebrews 10:38.) "The just" (the justified person, of whom only this can be said) "shall live by faith;" even now shall live the life which is hid with Christ in God: and if he endure unto the end, shall live with God forever. "But if any man draw back," saith the Lord, "my soul shall have no pleasure in him;" that; is, I will utterly cast him off: And accordingly the drawing back here spoken of, is termed in the verse immediately following, "drawing back to perdition."

"But the person supposed to draw back, is not the same with him that is said to live by faith."

I answer,

(1.)Who is it then? Can any man draw back from faith who never came to it? But,

(2.) Had the text been fairly translated, there had been no pretense for this objection. For the original runs thus: O dikaiov ek pisewv zhsetai kai ean uposeilhtai. If o dikaiov, "the just man that lives by faith," (so the expression necessarily implies, there being no other nominative to the verb,) "draws back, my soul shall have no pleasure in him."

"But your translation too is inaccurate." Be pleased to show me wherein. "I grant he may draw back; and yet not draw back to perdition." But then it is not the drawing back which is here spoken of.

"However, here is only a supposition, which proves no fact." I observe, you take that as a general rule, Suppositions prove no facts. But this is not true. They do not always; but many times they do. And whether they do or no in a particular text, must be judged from the nature of the supposition, and from the preceding and following words.

"But the inserting any man into the text is agreeable to the grammatical construction of the words." This I totally deny. There is no need of any such insertion. The preceding nominative suffices.

"But one that lives by faith cannot draw back. For 'whom he justified, them he also glorified.'" This proves no more than, that all who are glorified are pardoned and sanctified first.

"Nay, but St. Paul says, 'Ye are dead; and your life is hid with Christ in God. When Christ, who is our life, shall appear, then shall ye also appear with him in glory.'" Most sure, if you endure to the end. "Whosoever believeth in him" to the end "shall never die."

77. "But, to come more home to the point: I say, this text is so far from militating against perseverance, that it greatly establishes it."

You are very unhappy in your choice of texts to establish this doctrine. Two of these establish it, just as this does, as we have seen already. Now, pray let us hear how you prove perseverance from this text.

"Very easily. Here are two sorts of persons mentioned; he that lives by faith, and he that draws back to perdition."

Nay, this is the very question. I do not allow that two persons are mentioned in the text. I have shown it is one and the same person, who once lived by faith, and afterwards draws back.

Yet thus much I allow: Two sorts of believers are in the next verse mentioned; some that draw back, and some that persevere. And I allow, the Apostle adds, "We are not of them who draw back unto perdition." But what will you infer from thence? This is so far from contradicting what has been observed before, that it manifestly confirms it. It is a farther proof, that there are those who draw back unto perdition, although these were not of that number.

"I must still aver, that the text is rightly translated; which I prove thus: —

"The original text runs thus: 'Behold, his soul who is lifted up is not upright in him: But the just shall live by his faith.' (Habakkuk 2:4.)

"This the Seventy render, Ean uposeilhtai, ouk eudokei h yuch mou en autw o de dikaiov ek pisewv mou zhsetai, 'If a man draw back, my soul hath no pleasure in him. But the just shall live by my faith;' that is, faith in me.

"Now, here the man, in the former clause, who 'draws back,' is distinguished from him, in the following clause, who lives by faith.

" But the Apostle quotes the text from this translation."

True; but he does not "distinguish the man in the former clause who 'draws back,' from him, in the latter, who 'lives by faith.'" So far from it, that he quite inverts the order of the sentence, placing the latter clause of it first. And by this means it comes to pass, that although, in translating this text from the Septuagint, we must insert "a man," (because there is no nominative preceding,) yet in translating it from the Apostle, there is no need or pretense for inserting it, seeing o dikaiov stands just before. Therefore, such an insertion is a palpable violence to the text; which, consequently, is not rightly translated.

It remains, that those who live by faith may yet fall from God, and perish everlastingly.

78. Eighthly. Those who are sanctified by the blood of the covenant may so fall as to perish everlastingly.

For thus again saith the Apostle: "If we sin willfully, after we have received the knowledge of the truth, there remaineth no more sacrifice for sin; but a certain fearful looking for of judgment and fiery indignation, which shall devour the adversaries. He that despised Moses' law died without mercy under two or three witnesses. Of how much sorer punishment shall he be thought worthy, who hath trodden under foot the Son of God, and hath counted the blood of the covenant, wherewith he was sanctified, an unholy thing?"

It is undeniably plain,

(1.)That the person mentioned here was once sanctified by the blood of the covenant.

(2.)That he afterward, by known, willful sin, trod under foot the Son of God. And,

(3.)That he hereby incurred a sorer punishment than death; namely, death everlasting.

"Nay, the immediate antecedent to the relative 'he,' is 'the Son of God.' Therefore it was He, not the apostate, who was sanctified (set apart for his priestly office) by the blood of the covenant."

Either you forgot to look at the original, or your memory fails. "The Son of God" is not the immediate antecedent to the relative "he." The words run thus: "Of how much sorer punishment shall he be thought worthy, who hath trodden under foot the Son of God, kai to aima thv diaqhkhv koinon hghsamenov, en w hgiasqh?" You see hghsamenov, not uiov, is the immediate antecedent to the relative "he." Consequently, it is the apostate, not the Son of God, who is here said to be sanctified.

"If he was sanctified, yet this cannot be understood of inward sanctification. Therefore it must mean, either that he said he was sanctified, or that he made an outward profession of religion."

Why cannot the word be understood in its proper, natural sense, of inward sanctification?

"Because that is by the Spirit of God." From this very consideration it appears, that this must be understood of inward sanctification; for the words immediately following are, "and hath done despite to the Spirit of grace," even that grace whereby he was once sanctified.

It remains, that those who are sanctified by the blood of the covenant may yet perish everlastingly.

79. If you imagine these texts are not sufficient to prove that a true believer may finally fall, I will offer a few more to your consideration, which I would beg you to weigh farther at your leisure: —

"Ye" (Christians) "are the salt of the earth. But if the salt have lost its savor, wherewith shall it be salted? It is thenceforth good for nothing, but to be cast out, and trodden under foot of men." (Matthew 5:13.) "When the unclean spirit goeth out of a man," (as he does out of every true believer,) "he walketh through dry places, seeking rest, and findeth none. Then he saith, I will return: And he taketh with him seven other spirits; and they enter in, and dwell there. And the last state of that man is worse than the first." (12:43-45.) "And then shall many be offended; and the love" (towards God and man) "of many shall wax cold. But he that shall endure to the end, the same shall be saved." (24:10, etc.) "Who then is a faithful and wise servant, whom his Lord hath made ruler over his household? But if that evil servant" (wise and faithful as he was once) "shall begin to smite his fellow-servants; the Lord shall cut him asunder, and appoint him his portion with the hypocrites," (verse 45, etc.,) apostates, being no better than they.

"Take heed to yourselves," ye that believe, "lest at any time your heart be overcharged with the cares of this life, and so that day come upon you unawares:" (Luke 21:34:) Plainly implying, that otherwise they would not be "accounted worthy to stand before the Son of man."

"If ye continue in my word, then are ye my disciples indeed; and ye shall know the truth, and the truth shall make you free." (John 8:31, 32.)

"I keep my body under; lest by any means, when I have preached to others, I myself should be a castaway." (1 Corinthians 9:27.) "Our fathers did all eat the same spiritual meat, and did all drink the same spiritual drink: For they drank of that spiritual rock that followed them: And that rock was Christ. But with many of them God was not well pleased: For they were overthrown in the wilderness. Now, these things were for our examples: Wherefore let him that thinketh he standeth take heed lest he fall." (10:3, etc.)

"We therefore, as workers together with him, beseech you that ye receive not the grace of God in vain." (2 Corinthians 6:1.) But this were impossible, if none that ever had it could perish.

"Ye are fallen from grace." (Galatians 5:4.) "We shall reap, if we faint not." (6:9.) Therefore we shall not reap, if we do.

"We are made partakers of Christ, if we hold the beginning of our confidence steadfast unto the end." (Hebrews 3:14.)

"Beware lest ye also, being led away with the error of the wicked, fall from your own steadfastness." (2 Peter 3:17.)

"Look to yourselves, that we lose not the things which we have wrought." (2 John 8.)

"Hold that fast which thou hast, that no man take thy crown." (Revelations 3:11.) And, to conclude: —

"So likewise shall my heavenly Father do also unto you, if ye from your hearts forgive not every one his brother their trespasses." (Matthew 18:35.) So! How? He will retract the pardon he had given, and deliver you to the tormentors.

80. "Why, then you make salvation conditional." I make it neither conditional nor unconditional. But I declare just what I find in the Bible, neither more nor less; namely, that it is bought for every child of man, and actually given to every one that believeth. If you call this conditional salvation, God made it so from the beginning of the world; and he hath declared it so to be, at sundry times and in diverse manners; of old by Moses and the Prophets, and in later times by Christ and his Apostles. "Then I never can be saved; for I can perform no conditions; for I can do nothing." No, nor I, nor any man under heaven, — without the grace of God. "But I can do all things through Christ strengthening me." So can you; so can every believer. And he has strengthened, and will strengthen, you more and more, if you do not willfully resist till you quench his Spirit.

81. "Nay, but God must work irresistibly in me, or I shall never be saved." Hold! Consider that word. You are again advancing a doctrine which has not one plain, clear text to support it. I allow, God may possibly, at some times, work irresistibly in some souls. I believe he does. But can you infer from hence, that he always works thus in all that are saved? Alas! my brother, what kind of conclusion is this? And by what scripture will you prove it? Where, I pray, is it written, that none are saved but by irresistible grace? By almighty grace, I grant; by that power alone, to which all things are possible. But show me any one plain scripture for this, — that "all saving grace is irresistible."

82. But this doctrine is not only unsupported by Scripture, it is flatly contrary thereto. How will you reconcile it (to instance in a very few) with the following texts? —

"He sent to call them, and they would not come." (Matthew 23:3, etc.) "He could do no mighty works there, because of their unbelief." (Mark 6:5, 6.) "There were Pharisees, and the power of the Lord was present to heal them." (Luke 5:17.) Nevertheless, they were not healed in fact, as the words immediately following show.

"The Pharisees and Lawyers made void the counsel of God against themselves." (Luke 7:30.) "O Jerusalem, Jerusalem, how often would I have gathered thy children, and ye would not!" (13:34.) "It is the Spirit that quickeneth; the words that I speak unto you, they are Spirit. But there are some of you that believe not." (John 6:63, etc.) Therefore, that Spirit did not work irresistibly. "Ye do always resist the Holy Ghost: As your fathers did, so do ye." (Acts 7:51.) "Ye put it from you, and judge yourselves unworthy of eternal life." (13:46.) "While it is called today, harden not your heart. Take heed lest there be in any of you an evil heart of unbelief, departing from the living God." (Hebrews 3:8, 12.) "See that ye refuse not him that speaketh." (12:25.)

83. I do but just give you a specimen of the innumerable scriptures which might be produced on this head. And why will you adhere to an opinion not only unsupported by, but utterly contrary both to, reason and Scripture? Be pleased to observe here also, that; you are not to consider the doctrine of irresistible grace by itself, any more than that of unconditional election, or final perseverance; but as it stands in connection with unconditional reprobation: That millstone which hangs about the neck of your whole hypothesis.

Will you say, "I adhere to it, because of its usefulness?" Wherein does that usefulness lie? "It exalts God and debases man." In what sense does it exalt God? God in himself is exalted above all praise. Your meaning, therefore, I suppose, is this: It displays to others how highly he is exalted in justice, mercy, and truth. But the direct contrary of this has been shown at large; it has been shown, by various considerations, that God is not exalted, but rather dishonored, and that in the highest degree, by supposing him to despise the work of his own hands, the far greater part of the souls which he hath made. And as to the debasing man; if you mean, this opinion truly humbles the men that hold it, I fear it does not: I have not perceived, (and I have had large occasion to make the trial,) that all, or even the generality of them that hold it, are more humble than other men. Neither, I think, will you say, that none are humble who hold it not: So that it is neither a necessary nor a certain means of humility. And if it be so sometimes, this only proves that God can bring good out of evil.

84. The truth is, neither this opinion nor that, but the love of God, humbles man, and that only. Let but this be shed abroad in his heart, and he abhors himself in dust and ashes. As soon as this enters into his soul, lowly shame covers his face. That thought, "What is God? What hath he done for me?" is immediately followed by, "What am I?" And he knoweth not what to do, or where to hide, or how to abase himself enough, before the great God of love, of whom he now knoweth, that as his majesty is, so is his mercy. Let him who has felt this (whatever be his opinion) say, whether he could then take glory to himself; whether he could ascribe to himself any part of his salvation, or the glory of any good word or thought. Lean, then, who will, on that broken reed for humility; but let the love of God humble my soul!

85. "Why, this is the very thing which recommends it. This doctrine makes men love God." I answer as before. Accidentally it may; because God can draw good out of evil. But you will not say, all who hold it love God; so it is no certain means to that end. Nor will you say, that none love him who hold it not: Neither, therefore, is it a necessary means. But, indeed, when you talk at all of its "making men love God," you know not what you do. You lead men into more danger than you are aware of. You almost unavoidably lead them into resting on that opinion; you cut them off from a true dependence on the fountain of living waters, and strengthen them in hewing to themselves broken cisterns, which can hold no water.

86. This is my grand objection to the doctrine of reprobation, or (which is the same) unconditional election. That it is an error, I know; because, if this were true, the whole Scripture must be false. But it is not only for this — because it is an error — that I so earnestly oppose it, but because it is an error of so pernicious consequence to the souls of men; because it directly and naturally tends to hinder the inward work of God in every

stage of it.

87. For instance: Is a man careless and unconcerned, utterly dead in trespasses and sins? — Exhort him then (suppose he is of your own opinion) to take some care of his immortal soul. "I take care!" says he: "What signifies my care? Why, what must be, must be. If I am elect, I must be saved; and if I am not, I must be damned." And the reasoning is as just and strong, as it is obvious and natural. It avails not to say, "Men may abuse any doctrine." So they may. But this is not abusing yours. It is the plain, natural use of it. The premises cannot be denied, (on your scheme,) and the consequence is equally clear and undeniable. Is he a little serious and thoughtful now and then, though generally cold and lukewarm? — Press him then to stir up the gift that is in him; to work out his own salvation with fear and trembling. "Alas," says he, "what can I do! You know, man can do nothing." If you reply: "but you do not desire salvation; you are not willing to be saved:" "It may be so," says he, "but God shall make me willing in the day of his power." So, waiting for irresistible grace, he falls faster asleep than ever. See him again, when he thoroughly awakes out of sleep; when, in spite of his principles, fearfulness and trembling are come upon him, and an horrible dread hath overwhelmed him. How then will you comfort him that is well-nigh swallowed up of over much sorrow? If at all, by applying the promises of God. But against these he is fenced on every side. "These indeed," says he, "are great and precious promises. But they belong to the elect only. Therefore they are nothing to me. I am not of that number. And I never can be; for his decree is unchangeable." Has he already tasted of the good word, and the powers of the world to come? Being justified by faith, hath he peace with God? Then sin hath no dominion over him. But by and by, considering he may fall foully indeed, but cannot fall finally, he is not so jealous over himself as he was at first; he grows a little and a little slacker, till ere long he falls again into the sin from which he was clean escaped. As soon as you perceive he is entangled again and overcome, you apply the scriptures relating to that state. You conjure him not to harden his heart any more, lest his last state be worse than the first. "How can that be?" says he: "Once in grace, always in grace; and I am sure I was in grace once. You shall never tear away my shield." So he sins on, and sleeps on, till he awakes in hell.

88. The observing these melancholy examples day by day, this dreadful havoc which the devil makes of souls, especially of those who had begun to run well, by means of this anti-scriptural doctrine, constrains me to oppose it from the same principle whereon I labor to save souls from

destruction. Nor is it sufficient to ask, Are there not also many who wrest the opposite doctrine to their own destruction? If there are, that is nothing to the point in question; for that is not the case here. Here is no wresting at all: The doctrine of absolute predestination naturally leads to the chambers of death.

Let an instance in each kind be proposed, and the difference is so broad, he that runneth may read it. I say, "Christ died for all. He tasted death for every man, and he willeth all men to be saved." "O," says an hearer, "then I can be saved when I will; so I may safely sin a little longer." No; this is no consequence from what I said; the words are wrested to infer what does not follow. You say, "Christ died only for the elect; and all these must and shall be saved." "O," says an hearer, "then if I am one of the elect, I must and shall be saved. Therefore I may safely sin a little longer; for my salvation cannot fail." Now, this is a fair consequence from what you said: The words are not wrested at all. No more is inferred than what plainly and undeniably follows from the premises. And the very same observation may be made on every article of that doctrine. Every branch of it, as well as this, (however the wisdom of God may sometimes draw good out of it,) has a natural, genuine tendency, without any wresting, either to prevent or obstruct holiness.

89. Brethren, would ye lie for the cause of God? I am persuaded ye would not. Think then that as ye are, so am I: I speak the truth, before God my Judge: not of those who were trained up therein, but of those who were lately brought over to your opinion. Many of these have I known; but I have not known one in ten of all that number, in whom it did not speedily work some of the above-named effects, according to the state of soul they were then in. And one only have I known among them all, after the closest and most impartial observation, who did not evidently show, within one year, that his heart was changed, not for the better, but for the worse.

90. I know indeed, ye cannot easily believe this. But whether ye believe it or no, you believe, as well as I, that without holiness no man shall see the Lord. May we not then, at least, join in this, — in declaring the nature of inward holiness, and testifying to all the necessity of it? May we not all thus far join in tearing away the broken reeds wherein so many rest, without either inward or outward holiness, and which they idly trust; will supply its place? As far as is possible, let us join in destroying the works of the devil, and in setting up the kingdom of God upon earth, in promoting righteousness, peace, and joy in the Holy Ghost.

Of whatever opinion or denomination we are, we must serve either God or the devil. If we serve God, our agreement is far greater than our difference.

Therefore, as far as may be, setting aside that difference, let us unite in destroying the works of the devil, in bringing all we can from the power of darkness into the kingdom of God's dear Son. And let us assist each other to value more and more the glorious grace whereby we stand, and daily to grow in that grace and in the knowledge of our Lord Jesus Christ.

CPSIA information can be obtained at www.ICGtesting.com
Printed in the USA
LVOW10s2005301215

468476LV00022B/1222/P